SHORT HIKES
in Rocky Mountain National Park

text and photos by Kent and Donna Dannen

Tundra Publications
1997 Big Owl Road
Allenspark, Colorado 80510

Copyright 1986 by Kent and Donna Dannen
First Printing

All rights reserved. No part of this book may be reproduced without permission from the publisher, except by a reviewer who may quote brief passages in a review; nor may any part of this book be reproduced, stored in a retrieval system, or transmitted in any form or by any means, electronic, mechanical, photocopying, recording or other, without written permission from the publisher.

Library of Congress Cataloging in Publication Data
Dannen, Kent, 1946-
  Short Hikes in Rocky Mountain National Park.
  Rev. ed. of: Walks with Nature in Rocky Mountain National Park. c1981.
  1. Nature trails — Colorado — Rocky Mountain National Park — Guide-books.
  2. Hiking — Colorado — Rocky Mountain National Park — Guide-books.
  3. Rocky Mountain National Park (Colo.) — Guide-books. I. Dannen, Donna, 1949-   II. Dannen, Kent, 1946-   .Walks with Nature in Rocky Mountain National Park. III. Title.
QH104.5.R6D36 1986   917.88'69'043   86-16014
ISBN 0-9606768-1-3 (pbk.)

Maps adapted from U.S. Geological Survey Topographical Quadrangle maps.

Contents

Introduction 4

How to reach the Emerald Lake Trail and map of Bear Lake area . 7

NATURE WALK TO EMERALD LAKE 8

How to reach the trail to The Pool and map of the Fern Lake
Trail to The Pool 20

NATURE WALK TO THE POOL 21

How to reach the trail to Calypso Cascades and map of the trail
to Calypso Cascades in Wild Basin 32

NATURE WALK TO CALYPSO CASCADES 33

How to reach Fall River Pass and map of Fall River Pass area ... 43

TUNDRA NATURE WALK FROM FALL RIVER PASS 44

How to reach the Green Mountain Trail and map of Green
Mountain Trail 56

NATURE WALK TO BIG MEADOWS 57

OTHER SHORT HIKES 64

salsify seedhead

Introduction

Walking for Fun

"Arise, walk through the length and the breadth of the land," God told Abram. (Genesis 13:17). Modern Americans are following this command, for walking is our most popular form of outdoor recreation. The number of days Americans spend on trails has increased 16-fold in recent decades. Hikers have increased in number five times faster than the population as a whole. About $400 million worth of hiking and backpacking equipment is sold in America each year.

National parks in the West serve a high proportion of these walkers. Rocky Mountain National Park sees 600,000 trail users each year.

If you and your family or friends are not already part of these statistics, you probably will join the ranks of park pedestrians soon, or at least eventually. This book will increase your walking enjoyment in the park by introducing you to five short (less than two miles each) stretches of trail and the experiences with nature they provide. These trails represent the over 300 miles of trials available to hikers in Rocky Mountain National Park. Once on foot, you will discover why so many other park visitors also enjoy walking.

One of the reasons for walking usually acclaimed in reverent tones, is that it is *good for you*. For adults it builds more efficient hearts and lungs, and the physical benefits to growing children are beyond counting.

All of these claims are true, of course. But relatively few American adults do anything *only* because it is good for them. No children are so motivated.

The adults and children you meet on the trails are there for the fun of it. However, adults and children enjoy walking in the wilds for different reasons. Fortunately these reasons do not have to be mutually exclusive. And, at a younger age than you would guess, the kids' reasons begin to veer toward those of their parents.

For instance, most adults prefer to hike in areas little altered by human activity because such areas are the prettiest. "Natural" and "beautiful" have come to be synonymous terms for hikers. The taste for such beauty is addictive, and adult enthusiasm for the sights of wild places is slow to diminish.

Youngsters, however, often don't care about such things. Their interest in scenery is directly proportional to how much water it contains; mud is okay; snow is great! Fortunately, mountain lakes and waterfalls appeal to all ages.

We're not sure when children's fascination with water begins to wane; we're not that old yet. Actually, at what age young hikers begin to appreciate their parents' vision of wild beauty varies tremendously. It seems to depend, in large measure, on how early the parents baptize their kids in trail experiences. Stories of children as young as seven developing a sense of the beauty in nature are common among bold parents who begin carrying their tots into the wilds before they can walk. Bolder yet are parents who take the kids along when they barely can walk.

Another joy that adults experience while hiking is learning about all the interesting things that go on in nature. Many of nature's greatest wonders are tiny in size and invisible at a car's speed. Hikers discover processes of nature, color patterns, textures, smells, and sounds that are missed by nonwalkers.

Walking with Children

Children can help you to discover these wonders, for they force you to walk at a slow – very slow – pace. However, the passive pleasures of nature study usually aren't for kids who are beginning hikers. They are more interested in what there is to *do* – rocks to climb, games to play.

hiker in Glacier Gorge

With some imagination, parents can allow kids to have fun without wrecking the wilderness — a very real danger these days because of heavy traffic on some popular trails. Litter pick-up contests, with prizes for everyone, provide entertainment while teaching good wilderness ethics. Contests oriented toward nature — finding colors, counting types of plants, sounds, and smells — can be popular as well. The benefits of these contests to children are obvious. Less obvious is the fact that such games often benefit adults in much the same way.

After years on the trail, kids become as interested as their parents are with the more subtle joys of the wilds. Children are, after all, more limber and physically closer to many of the intimate details of nature. Children also are very nonchalant about getting dirty when creeping up on nature.

Even more than the facts they learn about nature, most adults value appreciation of and identity with nature. Here children start with an advantage over adults. On seeing a bird or squirrel or some other animal, an infant usually will cry out with joy. But the joy of sensing their relationship to the world's nonhuman creatures often is weaned away from children by life's other concerns.

Most adults unconsciously try to regain this lost joy. Those who succeed through walking often find that appreciation of and identity with nature provide their most profound joys and consolations. And parents bequeath a valuable inheritance to their children by introducing them to the natural world and by teaching them how to preserve it. Parents can thereby prevent their children from sadly losing their bond with nature.

You will appreciate all of the benefits of walking most if you keep your body reasonably comfortable. Even on short walks described here, wear comfortable shoes with rubber soles. Carry water to drink; do not trust streams. Even on a warm day, a jacket or sweater can become suddenly welcome in totally unpredictable mountain weather. Sunscreen is absolutely necessary for everyone, no matter how resistant to burning ultraviolet radiation he or she may be at lower altitude.

Walking in Rocky Mountain National Park is not the physically easiest walking you ever will do, although none of the trails we describe are hard. However, you never will find easier places to revel in wild beauty, uncover interesting natural wonders, or reestablish your identity with nature. Walking here will infect you quickly with an insatiable desire to walk as much as you can wherever you are, "through the length and breadth of the land."

How To Reach The Emerald Lake Trail

The trail to Emerald, Dream, and Nymph lakes begins at Bear Lake. Its parking lot sprawls at the end of nine-mile-long Bear Lake Road. In summer the parking lot frequently is full. Before the advent of the Bear Lake Shuttle System, brawls were common between motorists who drove around and around looking for a parking space. Now you can deposit your car at a less congested site and use free buses to reach Bear Lake with your sanity more or less intact. The 1.8-mile walk to Emerald Lake should restore whatever portion of your nerves remain frazzled.

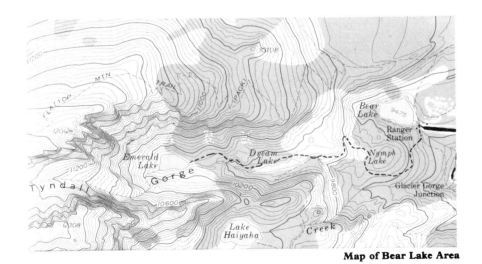

Map of Bear Lake Area

Nature Walk To Emerald Lake

There are two kinds of birds in the world. One kind waits politely to take its proper place at the dinner table. The other kind multiplies, fills the earth, and prospers by its own greed. Clark's nutcrackers, who never have been accused of politeness, fill the lake-spangled area below craggy Hallett Peak.

Most visitors to Rocky Mountain National Park enjoy nutcrackers because these large gray, black, and white jays are the least shy birds in the park. Their long bills are designed for extracting seeds from pine cones. But these aggressive opportunists also enthusiastically eat whatever can be scavenged from humans or other sources. Thus, your first greeting at Bear Lake parking lot may be a loud squawk from a flashy Clark's nutcracker, swooping by to see how the humans can be exploited today.

In 1805, William Clark, of the Lewis and Clark expedition, wrote the first description of this now familiar bird, which he saw along the Columbia River. Later named for its discoverer (who understandably mistook it for a woodpecker), the nutcracker's scientific name is *Nucifraga columbiana*. *Nucifraga* means "nut breaker," and *columbiana* commemorates the place where the bird first was found.

Usually raucous and rollicking, nutcrackers become silently discrete during March nesting time. To protect their young, parent nutcrackers sneak in and out of their nests, which resemble well-concealed squirrel nests. By June, however,

Clark's nutcracker

the fledglings leave the nests to pester their parents for food. Then both young and adults assume normal noisy nutcracker style. If the resulting din is hard on human ears, we can derive some satisfaction from seeing young nutcrackers bedevil their parents the way that adult birds harass us for food.

Nutcrackers frequently — and successfully — compete with gray jays for food at Bear, Nymph, Dream, and Emerald lakes. About the same size as nutcrackers, gray jays are just as bold toward humans. Both hungry members of the jay family share the nickname "camprobber." Gray jays have much shorter beaks and a soft plumage well described by their name. Their call is considerably more varied and appealing than the ear-splitting squawk of their more numerous nutcracker cousins.

A third jay commonly seen near Bear Lake is Steller's jay, an impressive blue and black bird with a long crest and white facial markings. Shyer than its "camprobber" relations, the Steller's jay is less timid at Bear Lake than anywhere else in the park. Like all other jays, however, the Steller's is a natural opportunist and will snatch any available food and fly to some safe branch. There he holds the morsel against the branch with one foot while pecking it into small chunks with fierce determination.

gray jay

Most walkers in the Bear Lake area enjoy these jays in warm summer. But the birds seem even more numerous at the lake when snows are 20 feet deep. At such times, when snowshoe hares are white and trails narrow to the width of a pair of cross-country skis, mountain chickadees join the flock of friendly birds here. With a bandit-like black mask across its beady eyes, the mountain chickadee is a typical mountaineer — somewhat scruffy. A bit larger than familiar black-capped or Carolina chickadees, the mountain version even calls a hoarser chicka-dee-dee-dee, as though just getting over a cold. In every other way — bouncing flight, trusting nature, general good humor, mountain chickadees typify their family.

Signs at Bear Lake guide the throngs of summer walkers to the trail to Nymph Lake. One of the most beautiful and easiest of park trails, it also is the most heavily used. Asphalt has been spread over part of the trail to prevent erosion from so many feet. Buck-and-rail fences in some stretches block off areas to allow nature's slow healing to take place.

You can avoid the crowds by starting your walk very early in the morning. Although not often a pleasing prospect, rising early has its virtues. Not only are temperatures pleasantly cool for walking, but also the sun's warmth has not had time to stir up convection breezes that ripple the lakes' surfaces. The reflections of Hallett Peak and Flattop Mountain on mirror-smooth water remain clear in memories long after the trials of early rising are forgotten.

Short-needled trees near Bear Lake at the base of the trail are Engelmann spruce and subalpine fir. Spruce trees have stiff, sharp needles which hurt when grabbed. Fir needles, on the other hand, are soft and painless to the touch. A less direct way to identify these trees is by their cones. Spruce cones are brown and hang down from the branches. Fir cones are dark purple to black and stand upright in the top of the tree.

When spruce cones mature, they open their feathery scales and drop their winged seeds. Cones of true firs fall apart when mature, leaving the cones' cores standing and still attached to the upper branches. Thus you will find no fir cones on the ground unless red squirrels have cut them down.

Red squirrels are common in all of the park's coniferous forests except among the widely spaced ponderosa pine at lower altitudes, but these bushy-tailed chatterboxes probably are most bold at Bear Lake in winter and summer. The scold of this little grouch is a familiar noise along most of the trail to Emerald Lake. But the red squirrel also is a ventriloquist. Although he keeps scolding as long as you are in his territory, it sometimes is easier to locate him by the sound of his claws on rough bark than by tracing his call. At the base of the Emerald Lake Trail, you almost certainly will spot a red squirrel and discover that the Colorado race tends to be more grayish brown than red.

As you walk up the trail to Nymph Lake, lodgepole pines soon become more common than spruce and fir. Lodgepoles have straight skinny trunks and gained their name because Indians came up from the plains to cut these trees for tipi poles. The two-inch needles grow in bundles of two and twist slightly.

Pines gained temporary dominance in this area when a forest fire swept through in 1900. Lodgepoles have adapted to fire. Their cones remain closed on the trees until there is sufficient heat to cause the scales to open. When a forest fire occurs, lodgepole cones open and immediately reseed the destroyed forest.

Lodgepole seedlings thrive on shadeless land cleared by fire. When the trees grow taller, they throw protective shade on spruce and fir seedlings. The short-needled trees eventually will grow tall enough to cut off the pines from light and crowd them out of the subalpine vegetation zone. Ironically, then, mature lodgepoles must die in a forest fire if the species is to survive.

Observant walkers may notice another type of pine as they near Nymph Lake – limber pine. Scattered on rocky or dry sites, these hardiest of mountaineers are distinguished from lodgepoles by bundles of five needles, which give limber branches a scrub bush appearance. There is a fine grove of limber pine on the north edge of Nymph Lake, but the most dramatic individuals grow on the blustery rock shores of Dream and Emerald lakes.

Early in the morning a wide-angle lens will be useful to photograph the reflection of Hallett Peak and Flattop Mountain (anything but flat from here) among the lily pads on Nymph, still shadowed by the surrounding forest. A normal focal length lens, however, will suffice on the walk around the lake, where Thatchtop Mountain is framed by burned limber pine. Longs Peak, framed by living lodgepole pine and subalpine fir, can be shot from a bit farther up the hill. The patterns etched by the wind in upturned tree roots probably are best shot in afternoon sunshine, if you can get it; cloudy skies after 1:00 p.m. are common.

Hallett Peak and Bear Lake

Although you can expect to see golden-mantled ground squirrels (face with no stripes) and smaller chipmunks (sharply striped face and back) scampering along the trail and red squirrels scolding from the trees, few hikers see nymphs at Nymph Lake. These beautiful female deities of ancient mythology are presumed extinct, having lost their habitat in men's imaginations.

But other nymphs, far from beautiful, abound in the pond. On the silty bottom, under lily pads, among stems of water grasses, countless nymphs—immature insects of various species—hide. Those that are not eaten by some predator further up the food chain will pass on to the next stage of metamorphosis, from nymph to adult, in a few months. Like mythical nymphs, insect nymphs are seldom seen. Their survival depends in large measure on being inconspicuous.

Nymph Lake itself is an example of metamorphosis. It is gradually silting in, becoming less lake and more marsh. The marsh will later become a meadow and eventually a forest. This process, called ecological succession, may take several centuries.

Nymph Lake was named when the flower floating on its surface bore the botanical name of *Nymphaea polysepala*. For reasons that doubtless seemed logical to taxonomists, this name subsequently was changed to *Nuphar polysepalum*. However, the lake retained its original name.

From rock outcrops above Nymph, you can look down on Bear Lake and beyond, along the ridge of Bierstadt Moraine to Sprague Lake and further to the three cliffs of Teddys Teeth atop Rams Horn Mountain. Named by early campers at the YMCA of the Rockies, the cliffs of Teddys Teeth were reminders of Theodore Roosevelt's full smile as portrayed in editorial cartoons in the century's first decade. Sprague Lake is artificial, built for fishing by an early innkeeper in front of his now razed log lodge. Bear Lake, on the other hand, is natural, as is Bierstadt Moraine—the lake formed by glaciers ripping up rock, the ridge formed by glaciers depositing rock.

Past this overlook the asphalt runs out, but thousands of hikers have tramped a trail that differs little from pavement. Here the slopes are more open and grassy. Among the rocks are brilliantly colored wildflowers—red Indian paintbrush, yellow arnica, purple larkspur.

Just past the stretch which looks down on Nymph, the trail rounds a bend and levels out. From here your eye is drawn to the square-topped tower of Longs Peak and the rugged Keyboard of the Winds rising above Glacier Gorge. Although there are no glaciers in Glacier Gorge now, evidence of their work is obvious.

The most recent period of significant glaciation began about 27,000 years ago, only yesterday in geological time. Our present warm period probably is merely a few pleasant millennia between glacial stages. Glaciers begin to form when more snow falls in winter than melts in summer. The most snow accumulates just below high passes where it is dumped by winter gales. At these headwalls, ice forms under pressure from many feet of heavy snow.

At last the ice becomes so thick and heavy that it becomes a viscous fluid, and gravity pulls it down the valley. As a glacier moves, it reshapes surrounding

Longs Peak and Nymph Lake

mountain slopes. Summer meltwater seeps into cracks in bedrock beneath and beside the glacier and refreezes there when temperatures cool. Expanding in the cracks, the ice wedges bits and block of stone from the bedrock. The glacier then plucks them away as it flows, and they become frozen into it. Drastic plucking occurs where the glacier has been at work longest, at the headwall. There steep bowl-shaped basins called cirques are carved out. Several cirques are visible in upper Glacier Gorge.

Other rocks are weathered off slopes above the glacier. They fall onto the moving ice, are incorporated into its bulk, and are carried down the valley as though on a conveyor belt. All this rock makes the sides of the glacier very rough. Rasping and plucking as it flows, the glacier widens the valley floor and steepens the walls, reshaping the valley from a river-carved V into a U. At the same time, it scours basins in the valley floor. Lakes in Glacier Gorge are water-filled basins which were scoured in this way, as are Dream and Emerald lakes ahead on this trail.

The trail to Dream begins to climb into Tyndall Gorge, from which one branch of the Glacier Gorge glacier flowed. Although Tyndall Creek is hidden by trees below the path, you can hear it rushing over boulders dropped when the glacier melted. Much of the creek's water comes from Tyndall Glacier out of sight at the head of the gorge. The brook gradually grows louder until the trail meets it a bit farther upstream. (The winter route to Dream Lake, followed mostly by cross-country skiers, runs below the summer trail from Nymph to Dream along frozen Tyndall Creek.)

Circling around a rock outcrop, the trail rejoins the stream at a trail junction decorated in summer by a profusion of wildflowers. The bridge to the left heads for Lake Haiyaha, a mile away on the other side of a ridge. To the right the path continues for a short way to Dream Lake. The bridge offers the last good view of Glacier Gorge and Longs Peak until you walk back down the trail.

Unfortunately, some hikers pause here to drink from Tyndall Creek, which other hikers have polluted with illness-causing fecal bacteria. Another unpleasant bit of aquatic wildlife that may be spread by humans is *Giardia lamblia*, a microscopic protozoan parasite. The parasite is carried also by dogs (not permitted on park trails) and by beaver and elk who picked it up from people. Some folks call the effects of this flagellate "elk fever." Some elk presumably call it "people fever." No water in the park should be assumed safe until boiled, chemically purified, or filtered through a special unit made for backpackers. Combining these techniques would not be an unreasonable precaution.

Dream is the park's most-photographed lake that cannot be reached by car. Photos of the lake with Hallett towering on the left and Flattop on the right might include limber pines in the foreground. (A wide-angle lens is helpful.) These pines are twisted into grotesquely beautiful shapes by winter gales that descend howling, ripping, tearing from the peaks. Dream at such times may seem more like a nightmare. But the rock-rooted limber pine (*Pinus flexilis*) survives by being flexible and gains beauty from tribulation.

Continuing along Dream's right (northern) shore, the dry trail rises only a few inches above the bog laurel and marsh marigolds. These marshy spots also are in-

habited by little red elephants. From a distance each elephantella looks like a spike of pink over wet earth, but a closer look shows that each blossom on that spike resembles an elephant's head. A unique warning often is heard here: "Be careful; don't step on the elephants!"

little red elephants

At the far end of Dream Lake the trail heads uphill again through a mature subalpine fir-Engelmann spruce forest bordering Tyndall Creek. Tall chiming bells droop over the creek, and Jacobs ladders nestle in shade at bases of trees. Jacobs ladder is named for the ladderlike arrangement of leaflets along a central stem. The ladder of Jacob, familiar from the Bible and from an American spiritual, stretched from Earth to Heaven in a dream the patriarch had while camping. Modern hikers may gain a similar spiritual uplift from Jacobs ladder and other trailside wildflowers.

The joy derived from flowers multiplies if you leave them unpicked; you can experience their beauty and leave it for other hikers to share. Wildflower pickers will get little joy from the fine they incur by violating park rules.

A ladder more substantial than Jacob's once was desirable on some stretches of trail between Dream and Emerald lakes. But trail crews have dug, blasted, and bridged until the path is easy to follow. Obvious signs of trail work can be seen near a huge boulder that dams a large pool in Tyndall Creek. Light-colored sharp rocks shattered by dynamite contrast with the usual trailside stones, tumbled and rounded inside a glacier and naturally weathered by wind, ice and rain.

The easiest passage is the natural choice of hikers. Before the trail was improved, though, hikers' opinions about the location of that passage varied greatly. As a result, a web of trails etched this narrow valley and increased the impact of hikers on the land. These old informal trails are gradually disappearing as nature (with some National Park Service help) repairs the damage. Walkers can help this healing process by staying on the formal trail marked by orange flags before the snow melts.

A few places in the trail still are steep, and occasional "photography" stops usually are welcome. One good spot is at a long banded slab of bedrock smoothed by glaciers and thousands of tramping feet. Tyndall Creek tumbles across the steep rock on the left. The moisture nourishes a belt of green, including some alpine lady ferns, in large cracks where soil has accumulated. It is particularly important at this spot to reduce wear and tear on the landscape by leaving and returning to the trail only on rock slabs.

Tyndall Creek and Flattop Mountain

The trail more or less levels above a wet and often flowery area on the left and then descends slightly — over snow until early July — to Emerald Lake. Twisted limber pine, spruce, and fir soften the rugged aspect of Emerald's rocky shoreline only slightly. Hallett and Flattop rise starkly out of the lake. Their summits cannot be seen from Emerald, but the visible spires and cliffs are more impressive than the summits. A wide-angle lens is essential for getting lake and dramatic skyline in the same photo.

Emerald Lake is a tarn, a water-filled basin scoured from bedrock by a stone-studded glacier. It is unusual in having no visible outlet. The water trickles through a wall of huge boulders, called a terminal moraine, which was dumped at the outlet end of the lake by a temporary readvance of glaciation.

Many hikers here are so enthralled by the cyclopean scenery before them that they neglect the smaller marvels at their feet. Be sure to notice the roots of ancient limber pine twisting over the bedrock and the chipmunks and golden-mantled ground squirrels scampering among them. The cheeping of friendly juncos (gray birds that show white outer tail feathers in flight) contrast with the piping whistles of yellow-bellied marmots who live in rocky rubble surrounding the lake.

Wind, usually welcome on a warm summer climb to Emerald Lake, will gust uncomfortably chill at lakeside. The breeze whips past snowfields on the far shore and skims an expanse of water that was ice only a short time before. But these perverse summer breezes are mild indeed compared to the gales of winter. Then a few cross-country skiers venture onto the lake ice for a different perspective of the place, glance briefly at cliffs shrouded by blowing snow, then hurry off to a less bitter environment.

The limber pine must tough it out for nine months of winter each year. Not only do gales bend and tear at the pines, but also they blast the trees with bits of rock and ice, ripping off bark and new growth shoots. But the scars and twisted grain form intricate patterns of divine artistry. Contrasted with this complexity is the simple drama of a root extending its form across a rock outcrop. The centuries-old bulk of a battered trunk sings with Psalm 66: "For thou, O God, hast tested us; thou hast tried us as silver is tried."

Walkers and skiers come to Emerald Lake, wonder, and retreat. But the pines cling constantly to the rocks in pride and joy. Preserved in a national park, they will endure and enjoy the wind until a glacier once more grinds inexorably down from the headwall of Tyndall Gorge.

limber pines

How To Reach The Trail To The Pool

Across Bear Lake Road from Moraine Park Visitor Center, a sign indicates a spur to Moraine Park Campground, Cub Lake Trailhead, and Fern Lake Trailhead. After following this paved branch for a half mile, turn left where a sign indicates. The pavement ends 1.2 miles along this road. Continue a mile past Cub Lake Trailhead to Fern Lake Trailhead at the road's end. The Pool is 1.7 mostly flat miles up this trail.

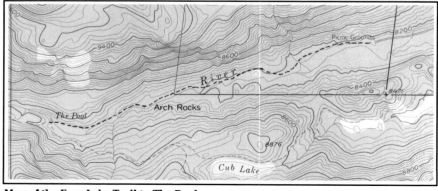

Map of the Fern Lake Trail to The Pool

Nature Walk To The Pool

"That sounds like a distress call."

We had paused in our hike along the Fern Lake Trail to locate the nest of a warbling vireo. Suspended inconspicuously in the fork of a quaking aspen, the delicate nest looked like a coverless softball cut in half. We were able to find it only by the vireo's unusual habit of singing from the nest.

To avoid attracting attention to vulnerable eggs or young, most birds perch at some distance from their nest before singing. But the drab warbling vireo apparently is determined to make up for dull color with a magnificent song. His exuberance while nest sitting seems to have no negative effect on breeding success; there are plenty of vireos around to repeat the performance every year.

Suddenly a far different bird call cut across the vireo's melody. It was a sharp, disjointed chirp repeatedly exclaiming, "Trouble!"

We watched carefully among the aspen leaves but saw nothing unusual. The call was coming from upslope, we decided, where lodgepole pines grew thickly among large boulders. There a robin-sized bird flitted around, perhaps diving at something, something that was swinging back and forth. It was hard to see through the trees; we changed position. The bird was a female evening grosbeak, diving at some object and voicing her distress call.

We climbed over the rocks until we could see a garter snake about three feet long hanging from the upper branches of a lodgepole pine, perhaps 25 feet off the ground. In its mouth was a bundle of gray down, obviously a baby grosbeak stolen from the nest. The snake swayed back and forth whenever the mother bird dived and struck it. Although the reptile was many times larger than its assailant, the mother bird was unafraid in her element.

We watched for 20 minutes to see if the grosbeak could knock down the snake before it could eat the nestling it had killed. But the battle seemed to be a draw, and we finally resumed our hike without learning the outcome.

Like nearly all humans, we instinctively sided with the mother bird. The long body of the snake hanging with the baby bird was repulsive to us. Had the grosbeak been killed by a prairie falcon, as once happened at our bird feeder, we would not have begrudged the hawk its prey (although we might have wished it had taken a house finch instead). To the mother grosbeak, however, there was no difference between snake or hawk, except that the hawk would be even more deadly.

The natural mortality rate for baby birds is around 60 percent, and snakes have a place in the natural balance. The value we place on birds depends on their not becoming too abundant, like pigeons, house sparrows, or starlings. The death of baby birds is assumed and prepared for in the abundance of eggs, so predators do not really reduce the total population of grosbeaks or other songbirds.

The chances to experience other complex interworkings of nature in the Big

Thompson River Valley on the path from Fern Lake Trailhead to The Pool are infinite. To experience events that broaden your understanding, it is necessary to slow your pace on this flat, easy trail. If you hurry, you cannot notice the countless interesting events occurring at trailside.

Notice the narrowleaf cottonwoods whose furrowed trunks surround the Fern Lake parking area. Together with chokecherry, ferns, and aspen, cottonwoods border the first part of the trail also. Cottonwoods occur on few of the other park trials, and in abundance only here. Like the familiar quaking aspen, the cottonwood is a poplar. It needs much moisture. The wood is soft, the leaves simple. It grows far larger than most aspen, however, and its leaves are so long and thin that they resemble willow foliage. The terminal buds are sticky and covered with five brown scales.

Cottonwoods are called "weed trees" by folks too rich in maples and oaks to know any better. Tree-poor westerners, on the other hand, know that the cottonwood is a tree to covet. Many groves of them are planted in hopes of fast growth and resulting fragrant springs, shady summers, golden autumns, and branches blown down to feed fires in winter. Overly fussy homeowners may object to the "messy" cotton produced by female cottonwoods to carry their seeds. But the tree's only significant fault is its reluctance to spread to drier areas away from watercourses.

In boggy areas along the river that are too wet even for cottonwood, willow, water birch, and thinleaf alder thrive. The shrubby birch and alder wall-in the trail where it is built up over ominous stagnant pools that look as though they harbor more mosquitoes than they in fact do. Encouraged by the swamps, birch and alder have extended their territory to the much drier rocky hillside above the trail (a habitat favored by the shrubby Rocky Mountain maple).

The water birch lacks the flashy white bark of its ornamental cousin, the paper birch. But the water birch has other familiar birch characteristics. Its leaves have toothed edges, and its bark is attractively marked by horizontal pores called lenticels. Like ornamental birches, the water birch tends to grow in groupings of several trunks and with drooping branches. Birch happen to far outnumber alder along this trail.

The thinleaf alder resembles a water birch but has a thicker trunk, stiffer branches, and larger leaves. Its bark is gray and smooth rather than reddish and lenticel patterned. Perhaps the most obvious difference is in the seed-producing organs, the strobiles, which are popularly called cones. The birch strobile is thin and falls apart when the seeds mature. Alder strobiles are woody when they mature, truly conelike. They grow in clumps on the ends of twigs.

A few yards farther ahead, solid land appears between the valley walls and river bogs to allow an evergreen grove of spruce and Douglas-fir to grow in damp but not soggy soil. The grove is an invitingly cool place to linger, even though you probably do not need a rest this soon. Before long a red squirrel, or chickaree (*Tamiasciurus hudsonicus*), begins the chatter it aims at everyone who tromps uninvited into his kitchen.

The layers of scales piled under these trees represent more than the litter from many generations of squirrels ripping apart cones to reach the seeds. This squir-

red squirrel

rel midden of scales is a cool, damp storage place for cones laid aside as winter food. The dampness, preserved by the thick shade of spruce and Douglas-fir, causes the scales of the stored cones to stay shut, preventing the seeds underneath from spoiling.

Each storage pit in the midden, or "squirrel's kitchen," may be as much as a foot deep and hold several cones. Other cones may be stashed in bogs and pools a few feet south of the grove. The squirrels must know what they are doing, for the cones of lodgepole pines, which do not open even when dry, are buried less deeply. You may even see them merely piled on top of the ground.

Neither lodgepoles nor ponderosa pines produce the shady areas needed for development of a good damp storage midden, so the squirrels transport cones here from other areas. They eat and store their food among Douglas-fir, even though these trees produce a really large cone crop only every fifth year.

Not only valuable to squirrels, the Douglas-fir is very valuable to humans as a source of lumber. It is economically important chiefly in the Northwest, where moisture from the Pacific fosters rapid growth and huge size. In the Rockies it serves mainly as habitat for wildlife and as decoration for the montane vegetation zone, usually on north-facing slopes or wet areas 6,000 to 9,000 feet above sea level.

The short soft needles of the Douglas-fir grow individually in all directions from the branches. Bark of the young tree is smooth and gray. As the tree matures, the bark becomes thick and rough. Perhaps the easiest way to recognize a Douglas-fir is by its distinctive cones, three to four inches long with three-pointed, feathery bracts extending from underneath the scales. In this grove tan thin-scaled spruce cones also lie atop the midden.

From the Douglas-fir grove, you climb a slight rise where the trees thin and a view opens to reveal Knobtop Mountain on the skyline. Knobtop is one of those grand peaks whose name is easy to remember when labeling pictures three weeks after you photographed the mountains. The round, gray knob which forms Knobtop's summit leaves no doubt as to how it gained its appellation.

Although rugged mountaintops sculptured by glacial ice are mostly hidden by bends in the valley and by trees, other effects of glaciation are evident along the trail. For instance, the valley floor is comparatively flat and wide, while the walls of the valley are very steep, especially to the right (north). After the mountains were uplifted five to seven million years ago, water flowing off them cut a valley with a narrow floor and walls less steep than today's – approximately a V shape.

When thousand-foot thick glaciers flowed slowly downstream 160,000 years ago, they began a reshaping of the valley which was continued by successive glaciers until as recently as 13,000 years ago. These masses of ice exerted their greatest pressure at the bottom, where rock was plucked and ground away from the valley wall. Eventually, the bottom of the V was widened, the sides were steepened, and the V shape transformed into a U. (The U shape is easier to see a short way up the valley or from the open spaces of Moraine Park.)

Other glacial signs appear in rocks dropped by the glacier when it melted between 12,000 and 13,000 years ago. The rocks were tumbled around inside the mass of ice and tend to be rounded, without sharp corners or edges. Glacier-dumped boulders isolated from their original location are called erratics.

Not all the boulders along the trail to The Pool were deposited by glaciers. Many are angular and piled together, the result of weathering which broke these rocks from the cliffs after the last glacier retreated. Yet even on these rocks glaciers had an effect. The steepening of the valley walls made the rocks more susceptible to falling. Long falls caused many to shatter into their present shapes. Rock continues to tumble from the cliffs today, but the rate of fall is slow. Today's milder climate reduces the rock-breaking processes of freezing and thawing.

Past an open field of chokecherry and creeping hollygrape, a stream from Windy Gulch trickles in branches across the Fern Lake Trail. Windy Gulch is an unglaciated valley a thousand feet above the path. The relatively quiet brook slackens its speed on the valley floor after a tumultuous plunge down Windy Gulch Cascades, out of sight from the trail. The same glacial steepening of the walls of the Big Thompson River Valley left Windy Gulch isolated high in the air – a hanging valley.

In wet areas where water crosses the trail, watch for yellow monkeyflower blooms, slightly reminiscent of snapdragons with red spots in the throat. Although common in other parts of the Rockies, the yellow monkeyflower is found only occasionally in this national park. Its name comes from the face that

Douglas-fir cone and needles

some people see in the shape of the blossom, thought also to resemble masks once worn by comic actors.

If you find the similarity of monkeyflower to comic masks difficult to see, take comfort from the absolute clarity with which the process of plant succession presents itself about three-fourths of a mile along the trail. Downhill on the left, an old beaver pond presents a classic example of how one type of plant succeeds another in a changing environment and alters the area further for the succession of yet a different kind of plant.

Beavers built one or more dams here, backing up the river around the roots of blue spruce and showing little concern for the beauty of what would become Colorado's state tree. Perhaps Douglas-fir and ponderosa pine also were flooded. The trees died and eventually toppled into the pond. Other dead plant material washed into the water, as did silt. Over a long period of time, the pond began to fill in from the upstream end, where the most silt settled first.

Water-loving plants took root in the shallow end, ultimately adding their own bodies to the filling-in process and catching more silt. Concentric rings of successively drier soil have built up around the edges of the shrinking pond. In each ring, plants adapted to that ring's particular moisture supply have taken root. Each year the pond becomes a bit shallower and the land around the edges becomes a bit drier. From the rise in the trail just ahead, you can look back (east) toward the pond and see clearly the successive zones of different kinds of plants. Blue spruces form the outside zone, water grasses and sedges the inside. The old beaver lodge is overgrown and almost hidden.

Eventually plants adapted to water will disappear. The blue spruce may be left growing only along the Big Thompson River. The lodgepole pine, ponderosa pine, and Douglas-fir growing in a mixed woods beside the trail someday may invade the edges of today's pond.

Past the pond, the view of the glaciated Big Thompson River Valley opens to display the U shape. The trail then descends and winds among large boulders surrounded by aspen. This is an excellent place to hear and watch for warbling vireos.

The trail takes on a particular charm and beauty among the aspen. Many of these white-barked trees have common root systems. They spread by suckers as well as by their cottonwood seeds. Their bark is a favorite food of beavers, who transform the soft, easily cut trunks and branches into dams and lodges. You probably have noticed new or old beaver-cut, conical stumps along the trail. When beavers fell the trees, more aspen sprout up from the roots or stumps.

When aspen trees remain standing for many years, they provide shade and protection for fir and spruce seedlings. Eventually these evergreens grow taller than the aspen trees and cut off their sun. This is another example of plant succession, and the beginning of it is obvious in this grove. When beavers cut the aspen, the grove survives. When the trees are allowed to mature and grow old, they are crowded out by evergreens.

Aspen bark also is a favorite food, especially in winter, of elk. Many of the black marks on the tree trunks resulted from elk stripping off pieces of bark with their lower incisors. The long vertical slashes blacken many aspen trunks from the ground to a height of six to eight feet — elk feeding level.

Unfortunately, the trees also bear less natural scars, evidence of slob culture in the wilderness. The soft aspen bark seems particularly inviting for carving by unthinking hikers. Ignorance is a valid excuse for some lapses of backcountry etiquette, but vandalism of trees does not merit such charitable judgment. Unfortunately, arrogant initial carving is frequent along this popular trail.

Nonetheless, aspen groves, which form green tunnels over the Fern Lake Trail in summer and yellow tunnels in fall, make this one of the most delightful paths in the park. The abundance of western bracken fern on the forest floor contributes to the overall loveliness. This species of fern grows all over the world, usually in sandy or rocky soil. In Rocky Mountain National Park you will find western bracken only in the montane zone and nowhere more abundant than here.

Indians used to eat the young shoots, or fiddleheads, of bracken fern — a practice which is, of course, forbidden to modern hikers in the national park. And because ferns are relatively rare in arid Colorado, harvesting them anywhere in the state is a poor practice. Besides, they taste very bitter and unpleasant.

Fern Lake was named for Fern Creek. A major tributary of the Big Thompson River, Fern Creek joins the river immediately upstream from The Pool. The growth of ferns along Fern Creek is unspectacular, though, and early hikers pro-

western bracken fern

bably had these western brackens in mind when naming the watercourse.

More than a mile from the trailhead, Fern Lake Trail winds beneath Arch Rocks. It is tempting to think that these giant monoliths were deposited by a retreating glacier, but they more likely fell from the cliffs after the glacier melted. After passing Arch Rocks, look at the cliffs above and note obvious gaps in the face from which huge rocks fell.

Growing around the base of Arch Rocks and in many other spots along the Fern Lake Trail is a shrub called waxflower, cliffbush, or Jamesia. Each name describes an interesting aspect of the plant.

Waxflower denotes clusters of creamy white blossoms with a very waxy appearance. A faint tinge of pink sometimes appears in the buds. The leaves are velvety and distinctly ribbed with an intricate system of veins. In autumn the foliage turns red — dark rose when viewed with the sun behind you, and brilliant stoplight red when the leaves are backlighted.

Cliffbush makes note of its typical habitat, cracks in rocks or very stony ground. It is closely related to the saxifrages, plants whose name literally translates as "rock breaker." The roots of cliffbush contribute to the disintegration of the rocks in which they grow. In fall—patches of red leaves shining from high on a cliff face mark the presence of cliffbush.

Jamesia commemorates Dr. Edwin James, a physician and botanist in the 1820 exploratory expedition of Louisiana Territory led by Major Stephen Long. James kept detailed journals of the expedition and wrote the first description of what later would be called Longs Peak, highest in the national park. He was the first botanist to describe many Rocky Mountain plants such as Colorado blue columbine (now the state flower) and several alpine species. He saw the beautiful tundra flowers on Pikes Peak when he and two friends made the first ascent. Returning from the climb, the three men discovered that their untended campfire had started a forest fire and burned up their food and equipment; this event gave them another, less admirable recorded first.

Past Arch Rocks, lodgepole pine is the dominant tree for the remainder of the way to The Pool. Typical of sunny and dry south-facing slopes, the lodgepole thrives in a dense stand. These trees generally sprout in areas cleared by forest fire, but other types of disturbances (avalanche or lumbering for example) can bring about the same result.

At The Pool, steep rock walls confine the Big Thompson River as it swirls around a bend; the swirling action has carved a pool in the rock. You can view The Pool easily from a substantial log bridge extending over it, but an even better viewpoint is available from the rocks a few yards along the west bank upstream from the bridge.

The Pool is one of the most dependable places in the national park to see water ouzels, or dippers. These gray wren-shaped birds, a little smaller than robins, perform a funny bobbing dance which gave them their name. They dive repeatedly into white roaring rapids to search for small water-dwelling animals, primarily larvae, to eat.

Hikers watching from the bridge and banks often believe that the bold ouzel has drowned in the turbulent river. But it invariably emerges, launching itself

mule deer fawn beside Big Thompson River

from beneath the surface to light on a wet rock, log, or ledge in The Pool's spray. Small wonder that this bird of western mountain waters is a favorite with hikers despite its drab features. Hours can be spent watching its brave and unconcerned antics at The Pool.

Nearly every summer a pair of ouzels builds a dome-shaped nest of moss on a rock ledge at The Pool. The birds enter the nest, somewhat smaller than a volleyball, from a hole on the side facing the stream. Usually the nest site is easy to observe but nearly impossible to approach over the protection of fast-flowing water.

Dippers never leave their streams and lakes for dry land. As top predators in their watery world, they have no significant enemies. Their intrepid dives and their humorous dances remind us that dippers and humans share the freedom which comes from living on top of the food chains in our respective worlds.

water ouzel

How To Reach The Trail To Calypso Cascades

Calypso Cascades flow in Wild Basin, south of the village of Meeker Park. To reach Wild Basin, leave Colorado Highway 7 at the exit to Wild Basin Ranger Station. A sign marks a right turn on a narrow unpaved road that penetrates Wild Basin for two miles to the trailhead. The fairly level trail to Calypso Cascades winds 1.5 miles along North St. Vrain Creek, a lovely white-water stream. After crossing the creek on a substantial bridge, the path climbs a moderate grade to the cascades, 1.8 miles from the trailhead.

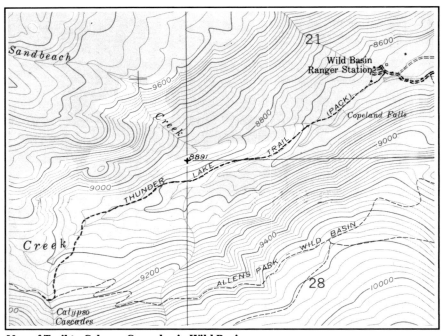

Map of Trail to Calypso Cascades in Wild Basin

Nature Walk To Calypso Cascades

In 1917 *The Denver Post* featured photos of a "modern Eve" venturing alone into Wild Basin to prove that a modern girl could survive the rigors of the wilds. Her total burden of clothing and equipment consisted of a leopard skin. This attire was brief by 1917 standards but may have provided more protection from sunburn or wind chill than many costumes worn in the wilds today.

Subsequent newspaper stories related Eve's adventures, which included serving wild foods to the park superintendent and Enos Mills, a local conservationist whose efforts to bring about establishment of Rocky Mountain National Park had succeeded only two years earlier. The luncheon menu consisted of pine bark soup, mountain trout, mushrooms, chipmunk peas, wild honey, and chokecherries. After about a week of wilderness living, the stories said, Eve had to be rescued by gallant park rangers from who-knows-what fate at the hands of a pursuing "Adam." Adam was clad in a bearskin and was known to the rangers as "the Crazy Greek."

Of course the whole thing was a hoax, attributed to the superintendent, to publicize the park and attract more visitors. Since 1917, much has changed in park management philosophy. Women personnel do not wear leopard-skin uniforms. And with millions of visitors annually, the park superintendent's main problem is how to keep crowds from trampling the park to death.

Yet Wild Basin is just as natural as when Eve served lunch a few miles up the trail. Pines still flourish, although any soup made from their bark would be relished only by porcupines. Mushrooms can be excellent, insipid, or a deadly poisonous food. Chokecherries are common a short way up the trail. Although raw chokecherries are tasty only to wildlife, chokecherry jelly tastes superb to humans.

Common wildlife in Wild Basin include mule deer and elk and smaller mammals such as chipmunks, golden-mantled ground squirrels, red squirrels, and snowshoe hares. Of the wide variety of birds, mountain chickadees may be most conspicuous. In winter, when cross-country skiers follow the unplowed section of road to the trailhead, chickadees are bold and numerous; one might even land on a skier's head or pole grip during the bird's ceaseless flutter from perch to perch in the winter woods.

Ski tracks and the hiking trail follow the same route from the trailhead, bridging Hunters Creek. In summer the fairly flat meadows past the bridge are filled with

chipmunk

flowers — golden banner, western wallflower, Colorado loco early in the season; yellow stonecrop, harebell, and asters later. In lodgepole pine woods a bit farther on, look for orchids — fairy slipper, or calypso, in June and spotted coralroot in July. Colorado blue columbine and arnica grow in the shade at trailside.

Wild rose also is common along the trail. Its bright pink blossoms are followed by bright red fruits — rose hips much praised for their high vitamin C content. Had Eve included these in her luncheon in sufficient quantity, she would have been protected from colds, despite her skimpy attire. But she would have added nothing to her reputation as a wilderness gourmet. Though often collected for use in herb teas, rose hips are nearly as tasty as bland mealy apples and are filled with annoying hairy seeds.

After crossing a few intermittent streams on footbridges, you will reach Copeland Falls, about a quarter mile from the trailhead. Copeland Falls amounts to a somewhat sudden drop in North St. Vrain Creek, a few yards to the left of the trail. It is worth a picture (best light is in the morning) but no more spectacular than several other unnamed places along the creek, which the trail follows for the next mile.

Up the hill across the trail past Copeland Falls, watch for pines with orange-brown bark and needles five inches long. These are ponderosa pines, the dominant tree of the montane zone of vegetation. Here at 8,500 feet above sea level, these trees grow near the upper edge of the zone, which extends as high as 9,000 feet.

The slow-growing ponderosas have dark gray bark until they are more than 150 years old. The deeply grooved orange brown bark takes centuries to develop, and the bark may be from two to four inches thick. It serves as armor against the heat of possible fires on the forest floor. But even thick bark is no protection against an attack of mountain pine beetles, deadly to a tree that otherwise would live from 300 to 500 years.

In a sunny meadow below the ponderosas are Eve's chokecherry bushes. This wild cherry (*Prunus virginiana*) grows throughout most of the United States. Its aromatic white flower clusters, almost overwhelmingly sweet, develop into masses of dark purple or black cherries that attract swarms of birds and jelly makers. In fall chokecherry leaves turn orange-red.

Missing from Eve's mythical menu were the berrylike blue cones of dwarf juniper (*Juniperus communis*), a low evergreen shrub with short sharp needles. Juniper berries are not tasty, but some walkers may find their aroma familiar: they are used to flavor gin.

Familiar to everyone is the shape of leaves growing on shrubs anchored among rocks along the trail. The Rocky Mountain maple is a stunted poor relation of a noble and valuable family, but it should be

mariposa lily

mule deer doe and yarrow

cherished as the only maple in the park. It tolerates excessive dryness and impoverished soil that quickly would kill big showy maples. In size and shape, the Rocky Mountain maple reflects the austerity of the arid West. Yet its vibrant red and yellow fall foliage indicates its relationship to the East's magnificent sugar maple.

Watch for beaver cuttings — conical stumps — a short distance ahead where the trail runs only a few feet from the creek. As of this writing there are few signs of fresh beaver activity, but beavers are notorious for turning up suddenly and changing the landscape to suit themselves.

Certainly beavers have been here in the past. North St. Vrain Creek is named for a fur trader who dealt in beaver pelts. In 1840 the first description of an area that might have been Wild Basin was made by a beaver trapper. In the 1840's, mountain man Kit Carson is said to have built a cabin just north of here on Cabin Creek as a temporary base for accumulation of beaver pelts.

During the colonial period the pelt of the beaver, the largest North American rodent, was used for making the finest hats. So great was the economic value of the beaver fur trade that many wars were fought to control it. The American Revolution had among its causes grievances arising from the exploitation of the beaver resource. This wild animal has helped shape American history and would be a fitting national symbol, except that the Canadians astutely laid claim to it first.

ski touring in Wild Basin

The sound of the stream drowns out most bird songs along this stretch of trail. But watch for mountain chickadees, warbling vireos, ruby-crowned kinglets, and Williamson's sapsuckers. It will be hard to miss the piles of cone scales stripped by the very common red squirrels seeking the seeds underneath. Occasionally you will see also a thoughtless hiker's attempt at immortality — a carving on a pale aspen trunk.

Beyond a section of trail that sometimes is wet from springs up the hill, you will circumvent a huge boulder resting on the end of an expansive bedrock slab sloping up from the creek. This monstrous rock was carried here by a glacier that flowed in Wild Basin about 13,000 years ago. Filling the valley about 1,000 feet deep, the river of ice moved incalculable tons of debris — boulders like this as well as microscopic dust — from the peaks and valley walls and dumped them at the melting point along the park's eastern boundary.

The ice's great weight concentrated on the valley floor, where all soil was stripped away and the underlying rock abraded smooth. In the 12,000 years since the glacier melted, a thin mantle of soil has redeveloped over most of Wild Basin, except where prevented by constant erosion on steep bedrock surfaces. Where soil has not collected, weather has eaten away the rock surface to make rough what the glacier had smoothed.

To feel the difference between glacial polish and weathered roughness, run your fingers over the cool rock underneath the huge boulder which has protected the surface beneath it from the elements. Then feel the sun-warmed bedrock along the trail. You can see the difference easily, but touching conveys a less abstract sense of the erosive power of weather over the last 12 millenia. Eventually, in lengths of time beyond human comprehension, this erosion will accomplish the vision of Isaiah:

> Every valley shall be lifted up,
> and every mountain and hill be made low;
> the uneven ground shall become level,
> and the rough places a plain.

On the other side of the bedrock slab, the trail penetrates a nearly pure stand of lodgepole pine; hollygrape appears on tne forest floor. Though neither a holly nor a grape, this low shrub is recognizable by its hollylike leaves, yellow blossoms in June and July, and blue berries in August and September. The berries make good jelly, though it is difficult to acquire enough for a recipe except in the Pacific Northwest, where a similar species reaches shrub size with a greater profusion of berries.

A favorite site for wilderness walkers or cross-country skiers to dip into their packs for food is where the path crosses North St. Vrain Creek on a substantial bridge. Photographers using shutter

creeping hollygrape

speeds of 1/125 of a second or faster will stop the spectacular display of rushing water with sparkling droplets hanging in the air. Resting your camera on the bridge railing and shooting at 1/15 of a second will blur the water into cottoncandy smoothness.

Past the bridge, the trail climbs fairly steeply above the creek for less than a quarter mile. While resting to catch your breath on the way up the slope, note the many large glacial boulders, one of which rests on top of another like a cap on a mushroom.

At a bend to the left, the path begins to level out. Here you can walk straight ahead onto a large boulder and look down on the junction of North St. Vrain and Cony creeks.

The trail follows Cony Creek upstream through lush forest where a deadly battle has entered its final stage. Engelmann spruce and subalpine fir have crowded out nearly all the quaking aspen. The biggest aspens in the park have made a magnificent, though futile, stand here. Old aspens with bark showing their cottonwood family lineage reach to unusual heights, as if striving to hold on to a share of life-giving light among the towering evergreens. Many aspen trees already are dead, and the rest surely will die as ecological succession grinds slowly but inevitably toward a pure spruce-fir forest.

quaking aspen trunks

stream detail

fairy slipper or calypso orchid

pika or cony

However, in 1978 the aspen here almost got a reprieve. A large fire, started by lightning, raged through Wild Basin. The fire jumped over a wet corridor containing Cony Creek, but spot fires burned not far from this stretch of trail. New aspen groves may rise from buried roots in those areas, where fire set back the process of ecological succession for a few centuries.

Listen for Calypso Cascades just ahead. In early July be sure to look down to the forest floor for pink fairy slipper, or calypso, orchids. Calypso was a sea nymph in Greek mythology, and this orchid seems to have a special charm. Wildflowers should not be picked in a national park, and probably not anywhere else. Nonetheless, thoughtless hikers too often pluck wild bouquets or single blossoms, which wilt at once. They then leave the dead flowers on a rock, log, or in the middle of the trail. But in the thousands of miles that we have hiked in this park, we have seen only one calypso so vandalized. Perhaps a sense of sanctity surrounds and protects the flower.

The stream cascading here is Cony Creek, but you will not see any conies nearby. "Cony" is another name for the pika, a round-eared cousin of the rabbit. Pikas dwell in large rock piles, mostly above treeline, common around Cony Pass and Cony Lake, where Cony Creek originates. Scampering through the spaces among their sheltering rocks, pikas are very active all year and never hibernate as other small mammals do. Instead they begin in mid-July to cut flowers, grasses, and other plants to dry in hay piles weighing as much as 30 pounds. They eat this harvest in winter.

At Calypso Cascades the trail splits. To the left it winds up to Finch Lake. The more popular trail to the right leads to Ouzel Falls and other destinations deep in Wild Basin. Both paths soon enter areas of heavy devastation from the 1050-acre Ouzel Fire, started by a lightning strike at Ouzel Lake.

Fire, though long feared by humans, is a part of a dynamic ecosystem. Mature

forest fire

revegetated burn: lodgepole pine, grass, cow elk

aspen and lodgepole pine stands would have been crowded out by spruce and fir competition had the Ouzel Fire not occurred. Now young lodgepole and aspen are repopulating the burned areas. Shrubby plants and many kinds of wildflowers, and the deer and elk that feed on these plants, also would have been crowded out by the thick canopy of a spruce-fir forest. The patchy pattern of plant variety in burned and adjacent unburned areas creates a variety of habitats for a wider range of animal life than existed before the 1978 fire. Burned trees provide interesting, unusual material for photographs.

But it is hard to be objective about the fire's benefits. We treasured the cool stretches of subalpine shade. We do not remember that our great grandparents laboriously cleared other forests to create their own and our feeding habitat — today's fields of grain. Instead we lament that no one alive today ever will see the burned 1050 acres as they once were.

It is this aspect of the national park which shows to us that great natural systems run in cycles, directions, time scales, and even purposes uncontrolled and unimagined by individuals, corporations, or bureaucracies. Contrary to our proud assumptions, the universe does not revolve around us. Good lessons frequently are not easy ones.

How To Reach Fall River Pass

In summer, Fall River Pass competes with Bear Lake for the distinction of being the busiest place in Rocky Mountain National Park. The pass is located along Trail Ridge Road, midway between Estes Park and Grand Lake. After the Fourth of July, the pass usually is accessible also by Old Fall River Road, a one-way uphill route which snakes for nine mostly unpaved miles from Horseshoe Park to the pass.

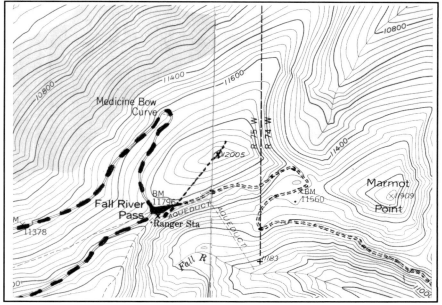

Map of Fall River Pass Area

Tundra Nature Walk From Fall River Pass

You are an alien in the liliputian land above treelimit. On this otherworld called alpine tundra (*tundra* is Russian for "land without trees,") you are a giant. Most of the natives are only a few inches tall.

Your summer embassy on the tundra is located at Fall River Pass. Here concentrate the greatest numbers of alien giants to be found above the trees. Here is nearly everything a giant needs – food, souvenirs, restrooms (remember, no trees), and National Park Service interpreters. Most important, the two fortress-like stone buildings at Fall River Pass protect giants from the cruel and all-powerful ruler of this world – Wind. None too fond of her own subjects, this despot fiercely despises foreign giants.

The Fall River Pass embassy exists at all only because in summer Wind mellows a bit and even departs occasionally from her realm. On rare and wondrous days when Wind is gone, her much-abused subjects and alien giants alike rejoice in the tundra's austere but vibrant beauty. Such rejoicing is all the more fervent because all know that Wind soon will return to lash lightly clothed giants, humbling their tall arrogance, roughly correcting their ignorance, destroying their comfort and – at her very worst – draining away their lives.

This is the tundra's ruler in her relatively benign summer mood. In winter, she gets downright nasty, and Fall River Pass embassy must close. Its staff retreats down Trail Ridge Road, fleeing the blows of Wind, who closes the road with deep snow drifts and her own formidable presence.

Then only adventurous giants trek above the trees. These bold ones try to hide from Wind, but they very rarely succeed. Wind usually is everywhere at once in her domain. She tries to kill all giants and occasionally succeeds. Unfailingly, Wind makes giants wonder why they ventured above the trees in winter.

Alien giants are attracted to the tundra in all seasons mostly by its expansive vistas in which a hundred giants can be lost to sight. Such scenes are sharp, contrasty, sparse, and so beautifully clear that far-seeing giants mistakenly think their comprehension extends forever through endless emptiness. More perceptive giants realize that the tundra is far from empty. They are drawn to the fascinating lifestyle of the natives – plants and animals – and their canny courage in surviving Wind's assaults.

Since so many giants congregate at Fall River Pass, the trail leading uphill from the parking lot has been partially paved and fenced to keep the multitudes of visiting giants from trampling tundra vegetation to death. Native tundra plants have a tough enough time surviving the abuse of Wind without having to endure repeated assaults from giant feet. One alien innocently treading after another has the effect of a brutal invasion.

battling Wind at treelimit

Ethical and friendly giants walk across the tundra as gently as possible. In less heavily visited areas where there is no trail, tundra travelers should walk abreast of each other, each giant stepping where another has not stepped in order to disperse the impact. Step on rocks whenever possible. In areas where a path already exists, however, walk in single file in order to restrict impact to an area already mostly devoid of life. At Fall River Pass more than anywhere else, DO NOT LEAVE THE PATH!

Do not leave the parking lot without warmer clothes than you needed below treelimit, where air temperature may be 30 degrees warmer. More important, the Wind in her tundra domain lowers the chill factor by far more than mere difference in air temperature indicates. Native tundra plants and animals avoid the worst of Wind's buffeting by staying low to the ground. Giants stand upright where they receive Wind's full blast.

Wind, furthermore, is fond of ambushes. Not suspecting Wind's potential presence, giants haul themselves and their children up the lower part of the trail. Wind then gusts literally out of nowhere to gleefully inflict misery and raise questions of child abuse by parents.

The cold air also is thin at Fall River Pass, 11,796 feet above sea level. Thinness means that the air contains less oxygen, both the O_2 that giants breathe and the O_3 (ozone) that blocks invisible ultraviolet radiation. Air thinness creates both immediate and deferred problems.

The immediate problem occurs when your giant body, starved for adequate amounts of O_2, compensates by deeper breathing. But your lungs still cannot take in enough oxygen, so an extra amount of blood needs to be pumped through them to carry O_2 around your body; your heart must work harder. Thus heart patients should be extremely wary of exercise at high altitude.

The deferred problem is sunburn. While lack of O_2 scorches your lungs, unblocked ultraviolet radiation scorches your skin rapidly. Most giants associate sunburn with hot air temperature because the two frequently occur simultaneously below treelimit. But UV will burn you in cold air too. While Wind is busy assaulting bare skin to inflict present cold misery, massive doses of UV are insidiously storing up misery of a different sort for later.

Of course giants differ in their sensitivity to UV radiation. But what you have learned about your personal tendency to burn in the sun below treelimit is irrelevant at Fall River Pass. Apply a good strong sunscreen (sun protection factor of at least 10) before starting up the path. Wear sunglasses to protect your eyes from both UV and Wind.

Wind has one very deadly weapon in her arsenal against which the only defense is hiding in the buildings or in your car. Lightning hurled from black thunderheads that Wind occasionally musters above Fall River Pass, strikes at tall objects, too often a luckless giant.

The path from the parking lot extends about a quarter mile up a hill to the north. Though not a long trail as giants walk, it is quite a journey in terms of tundra ecosystems. Also, giants find that trudging a quarter mile from 11,796 feet to 12,005 feet above sea level seems considerably longer than a quarter mile around the flat football field at home.

yellow-bellied marmot

golden-mantled ground squirrel

The presence of a permanent tundra resident is made obvious by dirt mounds piled along the path. The pocket gopher avoids Wind by hiding underground. No other burrower in the Rockies can match the pocket gopher's digging ability. The rockiest soil is no barrier to its strong, heavily clawed front feet.

One pocket gopher's burrow can be 500 feet long, winding from 4 to 18 inches beneath the surface. A gopher excavates about three tons of soil to build such a burrow. Side tunnels and chambers are filled with roots, and other plant parts stored for future gopher meals. Additional galleries are stuffed with feces or are used for nests.

So much digging affects the tundra greatly. Pocket gophers mix up the soil and enrich it with their excrement. But the mounds of dirt from their tunneling bury and kill many plants, in addition to the ones they eat. The soil then dries out and Wind erodes it, leaving lifeless bare spots where soil redevelopment may require centuries. Before Wind removes the loose soil, however, gopher mounds may support some of the tundra's most brilliant flower exhibits. Relatively tall, large-blossomed plants like alpine sunflower, alpine wallflower, and skypilot grow thickly in these "gopher gardens." Like nearly all tundra plants, these are perennials, but they live only a few years.

In some places melting snowbanks reveal twisting dirt ridges that resemble brown rope cable. Some of the more recent of these "gopher eskers" are two inches high; older eskers are flattened mounds, eroding or settling back into the soil. In winter pocket gophers tunnel through snowdrifts to gather dried plants while protected by the snow from Wind. Gophers dump soil from their underground burrows in the snow tunnels. This core of dirt traces the tunnel route after the snow melts.

Alien giants see pocket gophers rarely, for the little burrowers spend nearly all of their time underground. They have gray brown fur, small ears and eyes, and a short hairless tail. Their lips close behind yellowish orange buck teeth, which they use to carry soil and rocks. They are a little smaller than golden-mantled ground squirrels, which frequently are mistaken for large chipmunks at turnouts along Trail Ridge Road. Pocket gophers are named for their cheek pouches which are lined with fur and open to the outside; the gophers use them to carry food.

A typical pocket gopher has a perpetually foul humor and does not even like other pocket gophers. Except during mating season, they live solitary lives. (Pocket gophers live at all elevations in the park where suitable meadow habitat exists. But "gophers" frequently seen dashing across roads really are Richardson ground squirrels.)

Other wildlife species live on the tundra. Frequently seen in rocky areas along Trail Ridge and Fall River roads are yellow-bellied marmots. These western

alpine forget-me-nots

bull elk

cousins of the eastern woodchuck are on perpetual vacation: they sleep for eight months of winter and eat and sunbathe during the rest of the year.

Unlike the marmot, the pika works hard to harvest tundra plants to dry as hay, which he eats while remaining active all winter. A small round-eared relative of the rabbit, the frenetic pika pipes his barking call at intruders around rock piles, particulary at Rock Cut on Trail Ridge Road.

Bighorn sheep, elk, and mule deer, giants themselves on the tundra, appear along roads in early morning. Like human giants, these natives should retreat from the tundra in winter. But some tough sheep and elk have decided that they prefer to face the brutality of Wind rather than share the land below treelimit with increasingly numerous humans.

All bird species above the trees are summer residents except for an incredibly tough little grouse, the white-tailed ptarmigan. A rock-colored connoisseur of flowers in summer, in winter the ptarmigan sprouts white plumage, grows feathers on its feet to act as snowshoes, eats willow buds and twigs, and roosts under the snow to avoid Wind.

Along the path above Fall River Pass in summer, the bird most often seen by giants is the water pipit. This plain buff bird looks rather humorous when perched on a rock, bobbing its tail. Far more spectacular is the skylarking mating display of the male pipit. With an insistent one-note melody, he flies straight into

white-tailed ptarmigan in summer

the sky, soaring to distant invisibility unless silhouetted against a cloud. Yet the invisible singer still can be heard faintly as he hovers briefly before sideslipping into a plummet back to earth. He voices his rejoicing, ever-louder song all the way down. For pipits, song and aerial acrobatics appear to be the best defenses against intimidation by Wind.

Another particularly notable bird at Fall River Pass is the brown-capped rosy finch, usually seen picking insects off the snow. Although common here, this bird has a very limited range and is seen in summer only above treelimit in the Colorado Rockies. Rosy finches nest in cliff niches south of the pass.

Most of the path is lined by an alpine meadow ecosystem. Wind removes most of the snow that falls here by blowing it into the Fall River Valley, east of the pass. The early blooming flower here is the alpine forget-me-not, whose dainty blossoms appear in June. The white buttons of bistort bobbing on long stems appear later, along with western yellow paintbrush, mountain harebell, cinquefoil, and the dominant flower of the tundra, alpine avens. Other plant communities spotted through the meadow environment include gopher gardens and solifluction terraces.

icicles coat rose crown

Solifluction occurs when tundra soil is saturated by a permanent supply of water. Permafrost (frozen subsurface soil that does not thaw in summer) or bedrock prevents the water from draining away. Soil particles separate and lose their adherence for each other. They begin to flow gradually downhill, creating small level terraces on tundra slopes.

The solifluction terraces above Fall River Pass are not flowing now. They formed in wetter and colder times, possibly when a glacier lay on the east side of the pass where permanent snowfields lie today. Permafrost has thawed during the present warmer period between ice ages. There is some solifluction activity over bedrock along parts of Trail Ridge. Along this path, though, the terraces are fairly stable due to drier conditions and the bonding influence of plants, especially alpine willows.

Marsh plant communities form behind solifluction terraces and are easy to spot after the rest of the tundra turns brown. Supplied more constantly with water, the wet terraces stand out still clothed in bright green. Rose crown adds showy contrast to the marshes' green.

About halfway up the slope from the parking lot, the trail reaches a buried holding tank for the Fall River Pass embassy water supply. The necessary pipes are buried beneath the trail and are, in part, responsible for the path's existence. In the barren area where the tank was buried and along the edge of the path heavily pounded by giants' feet grow widely spaced fell-field plants. Unenriched by decomposing plants, fell-field dirt is not really soil, only small rocks. (*Fell*

white-tailed ptarmigan in winter

means "rock" in Gaelic.)

Nowhere is Wind more powerful than in a fell-field environment. With very slight plant cover to slow wind's speed an inch above the surface, Wind scours right down to the ground. It dislodges fine bits of loose soil and blows them away. It removes the protective blanket of snow in winter. As bright sun bakes naked fell-fields in summer, Wind desiccates the ground further. Even summer showers drain quickly away through the sand and gravel.

In this inhospitable environment, plants that survive are pioneer heroes. Often they are flattened hemispheric cushions – a streamlined shape that offers minimum resistance to Wind. Jeweled by masses of tiny flowers, cushion species include alpine phlox, sandwort, and dwarf clover among others. But our favorite is sturdy moss campion.

Although its narrow leaves give it a mossy appearance, moss campion is not a true moss but a member of the pink family. Its flowers are violet pink in color, and it is one of the easiest tundra plants to recognize. A deep taproot anchors the campion in shifting fell-field sand and gravel.

Not only is moss campion very pretty, it grows *relatively* fast for a tundra plant. A cushion a half inch in diameter may be five years old. Blooms may not appear until age 10 or cover the cushion until after 20 years. In a quarter century the cushion may near its maximum size, about seven inches in diameter.

As moss campion expands, it captures bits of soil from Wind and hoards them under the cushion's many-branched stems. Then cushions can be invaded by grasses and other flowers, which need more soil than cushion plants need. In the course of centuries, cushion plants may be choked out by invading meadow plants, and fell-fields may be converted to meadows.

The process of plant succession proceeds with almost geological slowness on the tundra. Look down the slope beyond the parking lot and Trail Ridge Road. The wide scar on the tundra marks the western route of unpaved Fall River Road between 1920 and 1932. The National Park Service strives valiantly each year to reopen the nine-mile eastern section of Fall River Road to permit one-way summer travel from Horseshoe Park up to the pass. But when Trail Ridge Road was completed in 1932, a section of the old road west of Fall River Pass was permanently closed.

Although the Park Service tried to blot out the old road and encourage plant growth, revegetation has been slight. Moss campion and its allies are doing their best down there, but centuries are required for plants to colonize lifeless fell-fields in the face of Wind's fierce opposition.

As you climb the path toward the rocks atop the hill, notice that meadow blends into fell-field. On top Wind is in complete control. There is practically no soil. Even cushion plants are few and widely spaced. Park Service interpreters have installed signs that name the surrounding mountains.

The path continues a short way beyond the top and down the other side to an overlook of the continental divide. Here another Park Service sign interprets the terrain. Below flows the Cache la Poudre River toward the Gulf of Mexico via the South Platte, Missouri, and Mississippi rivers. To the south Beaver Creek flows to the Colorado River and the Gulf of California.

moss campion

storm clouds above the continental divide

Many giants at this tundra overlook (beyond which you should not tread) are surprised to see the continental division of the waters 1,200 feet below them. But the shape of the land rather than its height determines which direction waters flow. Every drop that Longs Peak (the park's highest) rips from passing clouds flows toward the Atlantic. Trail Ridge Road crosses the continental divide at Milner Pass (10,758 feet), from which flow both Cache la Poudre River and Beaver Creek.

That the waters continue to flow at all in any direction after most of winter's snow melts is due in large measure to the tundra. Tundra acts like a huge sponge that soaks up snow melt and lets it trickle out slowly in late summer, just when Colorado most needs water down on the plains. Snowbanks on the high peaks melt slowly due to the chill temperatures at high altitude, acting as very efficient reservoirs for the thirsty arid West. Tundra covers 3½ percent of Colorado and supplies 20 percent of the state's stream flow.

That information is important to remember when you end your visit to the otherworld above treelimit. Once in the trees again you no longer are a giant. But you still have a giant need for huge amounts of water to drink, grow food, clean your body and environment, manufacture goods, process fuel, and carry waste. Many of these activities already are seriously restricted in the West by lack of water.

So the alpine tundra is more than a fascinating foreign environment. It also is an important source of one of our most basic needs. The natives of the harsh and beautiful land above treelimit are important allies, despite their diminutive stature. Both self-interest and simple politeness demand that as giant alien visitors we remember our responsibility to preserve and protect the miniature world of the tundra.

Wind's self-portrait in snow

How To Reach
The Green Mountain Trail

The Green Mountain Trail to Big Meadows begins on Trail Ridge Road about 3 miles north of the park's Grand Lake entrance and 17.5 miles southwest of Fall River Pass. One of the least used short trails on the western side of the park, the Green Mountain Trail is 1.8 miles long and passes through dense forest to Big Meadows, where views open to reveal the high tundra slopes of Mt. Ida on the continental divide.

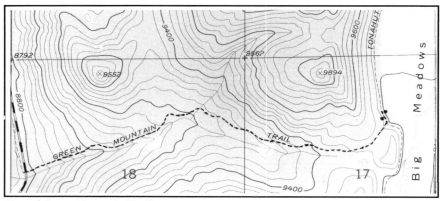

Map of Green Mountain Trail

Nature Walk To Big Meadows

"Crazy," his neighbors called him. "Sam Stone was nutty as a fruitcake," thought a turn-of-the-century housewife in Grand Lake.

But those who choose to live alone beyond the edges of civilization frequently seem a bit touched in the head to those of us who choose the easier life. What Sam's goals, dreams, desires, or ambitions were no one really knows. In any case, he tried to make a living by growing hay at 9,400 feet in Big Meadows. He plowed a portion of this marsh and built a wagon road to haul his hay down to ranches along the Colorado River.

Then he met a lady, a spiritualist, who divined that there was gold to be found in Paradise Park, at the southern boundary of what would become Rocky Mountain National Park. Sam Stone gave up his hayfield. With his spiritualist he ventured into what still is one of the most remote areas in the national park. The two never were seen again.

Likely nothing sinister or tragic happened. The lady was a poor geologist; if there was any gold in Paradise Park, it was in her teeth. The bogs, thickets, and centuries of fallen trees must have been very discouraging when combined with no pay dirt. Sam, with or without his spiritualist, probably moved on to the next range of mountains.

But his wagon road to Big Meadows remains. It is the Green Mountain Trail, relatively broad and smooth and easy to walk. This pleasant path to Big Meadows passes through some of the most biologically diverse land in the national park.

Most of the route follows the verdant course of an unnamed branch of Onahu Creek. The trail begins at 8,794 feet above sea level among spruce and aspen. These thirsty trees grow primarily where a higher than normal amount of water is available.

Many of the shrubs seen along the trail, especially where it borders the brook, are even more dependent on copious amounts of water. Alder and willow dangle their rootlets in the streams. Twinberry, a honeysuckle, displays pairs of yellow blossoms surrounded by petal-like bracts that later turn dark red and enclose two shiny black berries. Somewhat less thirsty are the creeping juniper and wild rose.

Another streamside plant worthy of notice is the horsetail or scouring rush. Aptly named, this 4- to 18-inch-tall plant appears to have no leaves, only a clump of green flexible stems branching from the stalk. Less frequently seen because they die off early in the season are unbranched stems, each bearing a single cone-like knob on top.

These two types of stems are both horsetails. The one that *looks* like a horsetail is an infertile stem. The unbranched stem is fertile; it reproduces from spores in the knob, or strobilus.

Holdovers from an ancient time before plants developed flowers and seeds,

Usnea or beard lichen

horsetails are closely related to ferns. Horsetails do have leaves, but they are reduced to tiny scales around the joints in the stems; those scales which bear spore cases make up the strobilus. The hollow jointed stems are green and contain chlorophyll, with which they manufacture food.

The stems also contain bits of silica, which prompt the plant's other name of scouring rush. Early pioneers used the infertile horsetail stems as scouring pads to clean pans. If you have a tarnished penny in your pocket, you can polish it with a piece of horsetail, demonstrating easily how well the old technique worked – in summer.

Gray green tangled filaments of Usnea or beard lichen hang from branches along the trail, another indication of the relatively high moisture around the stream. Usnea takes its water from the air and requires high humidity to survive. In this park, beard lichen hangs only in well-shaded areas of subalpine forest.

Related to crusty lichens growing on the rocks and leaflike lichens growing on the forest floor, Usnea is a fruticose or shrubby lichen. Among the most remarkable and widespread of plants, lichens are explained on nearly every nature trail in the nation. They are a cooperative intergrowth of a wide variety of algae and fungi. The algae, which contain chlorophyll, make food for the lichen. The fungi do nearly everything else, such as storing water and providing support.

Usnea in other parts of the world is used as fodder for animals. It also has been used in the past to treat a variety of ailments ranging from whooping cough to epilepsy. As long ago as 300 B.C., beard lichen was used to "cure" baldness. Some species of Usnea yield an orange dye.

Usnea does not seem to harm the trees but uses them only for support. It might kill a few needles on lower branches by blocking them from the sun, but these branches likely would be shaded to death anyway by the branches above. Usnea cannot live in the desiccating light intensity that needles use to produce food for the tree.

Farther up the trail, you pass tall pines with reddish bark, lodgepole pines which tolerate drier soil. Their prevalence outside the stream's course indicates

lodgepole pine forest

that a forest fire once swept the area. In a natural climax forest, Engelmann spruce and subalpine fir are the dominant trees. A climax forest will produce the same dominant trees theoretically forever until some outside force – avalanche, wind, forest fire, insect plague, beaver ponds, bulldozer – destroys the forest. Then the trees that naturally sprout will not be spruce and fir, which require much moisture. Outside of stream courses moisture is preserved for the trees by spongy forest soils that are kept from drying out by the cool shade of the trees. A fire not only destroys the shade, but will consume the soil as well.

Hardy, sun-loving lodgepole pine grow amid burned skeletons of the spruce and fir. The lodgepole forest along the Green Mountain Trail is very advanced in its development. The individual trunks approach maximum size for lodgepoles. They grow relatively far apart and are easy to walk among. Usually the lodgepole begin reforestation as skinny trees growing very close together in "dog-hair" stands. Over many decades dog-hair stands thin themselves when weaker trees die and make room for stronger trees to grow bigger and stronger yet.

Once these pines shade the ground and add organic content, the soil more readily retains water. Small spruces and firs are growing up in the shade of the lodgepoles. Eventually the spruce and fir will grow taller than the pines and shut off their light. The sun-loving pines will be choked out by thirsty spruce and fir.

Ironically, fire burning the forest again and killing all the pines would prevent succession of the spruce and fir, while keeping the pines dominant. Burned lodgepole would be replaced by more lodgepole. As it happens, lodgepoles tend to burn easily because they grow close together and produce a large amount of dead, dry needles and branches that are excellent tinder. Their cones have adapted to remain closed until opened by intense heat. After the fire has passed, the cones release a blizzard of seeds to start the proces all over again.

There are places along the upper end of the trail where it is too wet even for spruce and fir. These marshes or ponds were formed where glaciers 10,000 years ago left low places in the ground. The water-collecting depressions may have been formed by the uneven dumping of rocks and boulders carried by the ice sheets and deposited when the glaciers melted. The trailside rocks which appear as the path begins to climb were carried from the high peaks by glaciers.

Some kettleholes could have been formed when melting glaciers left behind huge chunks of ice covered by dirt, which insulated the ice and greatly retarded melting. More dirt collected on the blocks, perhaps to a depth of several feet, so that shrubs and trees grew atop the buried ice. When the ice finally did melt, the land above it sank, creating depressions in which water collects.

Walking away from the trail to the sunny edge of a marsh, you can see that it is gradually drying out. Water carries silt into the pond or marsh, dropping the silt first at the edges. Yellow pond lilies grow in the shallow water. (These are found in the largest, uppermost pond near Big Meadows.) In shallower water, which may dry up totally in droughts, are water grasses and sedges. Along the boggy edges are willows and alder. Over the millenia, spruce and fir eventually will grow where pond lilies float today – unless another glacier bears down first to wipe out all life.

Surmounting a last low ridge of forest-covered glacial debris, the path descends

marsh grass

beaver pond in Big Meadows

a short way to Big Meadows. Through this large open marsh, Tonahutu Creek wanders in a maze of channels. The parts of the meadow which have dried out a bit are the same spots in which Sam Stone tried to make a living by haying.

Two of his log buildings are five minutes up the trail to the left (north). The first building is his dwelling; its center beam is now collapsed, the walls are tumble-down, and pine and fir seedlings battle for control of the floor. At present the pines hold the lead.

The next building, a short way farther on, is a barn, its roof also caved in by heavy winter snow over the last 80 years. In such a cool and relatively dry climate, these buildings, like most human endeavors, are slow to disappear. There are few decay organisms to recycle dead plants back into the ground. Hence the soil receives little recharging of the minerals which growing plants remove.

In addition to Sam Stone's buildings, there are newer lodges in Big Meadows. However, they all have their entrances underwater and were built by beavers in ponds backed up behind dams across channels of Tonahutu Creek. (*Tonahutu* is an Arapaho word meaning, of course, "big meadows.") Willow and alder supply food and building material for these natural engineers who seem to fare better with their work here than Sam did.

corner of Sam Stone's cabin

There is no indication that Sam worked any less hard than the beavers do. But some creatures obviously are meant to reside in Big Meadows, while others are intended only to visit.

Other Short Hikes

SPRAGUE LAKE NATURE TRAIL is a nearly flat, .5-mile loop around the lake from a picnic area along Bear Lake Road. It provides many signs of beaver labor, entertaining mallards, and excellent views of the Front Range (often reflected on the still surface in early morning).

GLACIER GORGE TRAILS traverse a classic ice-carved spectacle from a parking area near the end of Bear Lake Road. Alberta Falls is set among quaking aspen .6 mile from the trailhead. After walking through an area opened by a 1900 forest fire, hikers reach a junction 1.9 miles from the trailhead where signs point the way to Lake Haiyaha (1 mile farther), The Loch (.8 mile farther), and Mills Lake (.6 mile farther). Mills and The Loch each have their backers as the park's most scenic lake.

BEAR LAKE NATURE TRAIL is a .5-mile paved path around the lake and emphasizes plants and glacial geology.

LAKE HAIYAHA is 2.1 miles from Bear Lake and is reached by a trail that splits from the Emerald Lake Trail at Dream Lake (page 14). Haiyaha is said to be an Indian name meaning big boulders; the lake is surrounded by giant rocks dropped by retreating glacial ice thousands of years ago. Lake Haiyaha also is framed by some of the park's most interesting limber pines. A path from the Lake Haiyaha Trail links with Glacier Gorge trails, permitting an interesting loop hike back to Bear Lake.

BIERSTADT LAKE is midway along a handy loop completed by the Bear Lake Shuttle, when it is in operation. A 1.6-mile walk from Bear Lake begins with an elevation gain then winds through the woods to Bierstadt Lake, a depression between two ridges of debris (moraines) laid down by glaciers. From the lake, another trail runs 1.4 miles across aspen-covered Bierstadt Moraine down to Bear Lake Road. Yellow aspen in fall frame wonderful views from this path, easily accessible from the Bierstadt Lake Trailhead even though the shuttle does not run in autumn.

CUB LAKE is 2.3 miles of wildflowers, birds, and other wildlife from its trailhead (page 20). Most of the way is relatively level, easy walking before the trail climbs through aspen and Douglas-fir to pond lilies on the lake. Not as awesome as the park's glacier-carved tarns, Cub Lake is nonetheless very lovely. A trail continues on to The Pool for a total 6-mile loop that includes a mile of road walking back to your car.

BIG THOMPSON RIVER OVERLOOK is 2 miles up the Old Ute Trail from the end of an unpaved road that leaves Highway 36 at .7 mile from the park's Beaver Meadows Entrance. Passing through meadows and forests, the trail emerges onto a fine vista where Windy Gulch Cascades tumble mostly out of sight 1,000 feet down to the river.

To Bob,
My friend
May God
paths of your journey!

Randy James

Unraveling the Revelation
Devotional Readings from the Apocalypse, written from an A-millennial perspective

Randy L. James

authorHOUSE®

AuthorHouse™
1663 Liberty Drive
Bloomington, IN 47403
www.authorhouse.com
Phone: 1-800-839-8640

© 2010 Randy L. James. All rights reserved.

No part of this book may be reproduced, stored in a retrieval system, or transmitted by any means without the written permission of the author.

First published by AuthorHouse   5/21/2010

ISBN: 978-1-4520-0784-7 (e)
ISBN: 978-1-4520-0783-0 (sc)

Library of Congress Control Number: 2010905848

Printed in the United States of America
Bloomington, Indiana

This book is printed on acid-free paper.

Acknowledgements

There are so many people that have contributed to the writing of this book. Included certainly are congregations I have pastored, which often offered critical insights by their questions posed in class settings and following sermons. I am also greatly indebted to my wife, Mary Jane, who has for years urged me to put down my thoughts on paper for others to read. Darlene Welch, a long-time friend and dedicated copy-editor, has painstakingly proofread my text and has offered her insights and comments to help make this book more grammatically correct and easier to understand. If there are still problems with the text, however, they are mine and not hers. She has done her work faithfully and diligently.

Most of all I am indebted Pastoral friends such as the late James C. Baker, my mentor following college who started me on this path and Dr. Philip Rogers, a Bible teacher and friend who help me to correct some faulty thinking long ago. These and many other soldiers of the cross who have helped to guide my way have blessed me. I trust that this book will be a blessing and tribute to them as well.

Dedication

This book is dedicated to my children, Toni and Rick, ministers of the faith and loves of my life, who taught me the value of passing on what I have learned to future generations.

Introduction

It has long been my dream to put down on paper what I have come to believe about John's Revelation of Jesus Christ. What is presented here is the culmination of thirty years of reading, studying, asking questions, and praying for guidance in order to put it all down in the form of devotional reading. In the course of this journey I have changed my mind about many things and have had to eventually come to grips with the fact that I will never understand this book as fully as I would like. However, I have learned much and this work is the result of my personal quest for knowledge.

It is my hope that this book will be of value to God's great mass of laity from all walks of life. It is written with this group in mind. That is not to say that some of my brethren of the clergy could not find help from these pages, but it was written primarily for the people who sit week by week faithfully in the pews. They have been my inspiration throughout a lifetime of preaching to them, teaching them, and trying to answer their questions. I will always be indebted for their support, encouragement, and challenges that have formed my ministry. With the laity in mind, the text is printed, but many of the scriptural references are not. This book is intended to be a guide and supplement to the Bible, which contains the real words of life, for my simple words are merely educated opinions. God's Word is alive and crucial to the study of John's writings. The Bible, where quoted, unless otherwise listed, is from the New International Version.

Because of this focus group, this writing will not be technical and it is hoped that the content will be understood without a great deal of theological training. Because this work is devotional in style and because it is a compilation of information that was gathered over a long period of time, I have been unable to document much of what is written. I realize that this approach is not very scholarly, but then that is not the purpose of this writing. I have carefully tried to avoid plagiarism, but if someone else's thoughts or materials have gotten mixed with mine over the years and ended up in this writing, it is not intentional. I apologize in advance if anyone has been slighted, for that is certainly not my intention.

My goal is simple. I want people to understand that this beautiful message from the Lord is for all generations of people. It is a book that inspires hope and a reason for faith. It is not just about "pie in the sky by and by," but about every generation of the Church of Jesus Christ. It is written for the last days, for it was written for every day.

The message of the book of Revelation in a nutshell is this: In this world the Church will endure hard places and hard times, but if the family of God will hold fast to the faith they have received, in the end they will win.

That is what I have learned as fact. The rest that follows in these pages is all commentary.

Randall L. James
April 2009

The Revelation

Prologue: Revelation 1:1–3:22	xiii
The First Vision: Revelation 4:1–5:14	45
The Second Vision: Revelation 6:1–8:5	59
The Third Vision: Revelation 8:6–11:19	77
The Fourth Vision: Revelation 12:1–14:20	105
The Fifth Vision: Revelation 15:1–19:10	129
The Sixth Vision: Revelation 19:11–20:15	163
The Seventh Vision: Revelation 21:1–22:5	175
Epilogue – Revelation 22:6–11	185

Prologue: Revelation 1:1-3:22

John is confronted by the living Christ while in exile on the Isle of Patmos (Chapter 1). He is instructed by Christ to write letters to seven churches in Asia. The introductory message to each church is as follows:

1. **Ephesus** – You are doctrinally correct, but you have walked away from your initial love relationship with people and with the Lord. Get it back or face the consequences. (2:1–7)
2. **Smyrna** – Although you are doing well, you are going to endure suffering. Hold fast to what you have received and you will not lose your reward. (2:8–11)
3. **Pergamum** – You have folks there who are faithful, but you also are allowing false doctrines among yourselves. Get it right or face the wrath of the living Christ. (2:12–17)
4. **Thyatira** – You are making progress in many areas, but you are allowing a false teacher to lead you. She and those who follow her are going to pay for their sins, but those who hold fast to the right way will not lose their reward. (2:18–29)
5. **Sardis** – Though folks think you are alive, you are really dead. You need to wake up and get right or Christ will come to you unexpectedly and you will face the consequences for your sin. (3:1–6)
6. **Philadelphia** – Though you have just a little strength, hold on tight to what you have. Jesus is with you and no one can stop what He does. (3:7–13)
7. **Laodicea** – Your lukewarm religion literally makes Christ sick. You think you are so high and mighty, but you actually turn His stomach. Let Him back into the church so that you can be restored. (3:14–22)

Pulling Back the Curtain

The revelation of Jesus Christ, which God gave him to show his servants what must soon take place. (1:1a)

One of the pet peeves that I have is hearing people refer to the last book of the Bible as "Revelations" (plural), instead of in the singular as it is plainly presented. It is not, nor has it ever been, a book about searching for what I call the "Christian occult," that is, secret messages that can only be discerned by specially gifted people who can interpret the images, numbers, and scary stories. It is the Revelation of Jesus Christ, or *The Apocalypse* (Greek), if one wants to get really technical. Its purpose is to reveal, but not just to reveal secret insights. Its overall purpose is to reveal Christ and the plan the Father has put in place for our world.

In this simple verse we see the deity of Jesus, the power of the Father, and the concern of the Godhead to provide us with information that would prepare us for consistent Christian living. The Father wants us to have all the data that we need to carry out the mission the Son left for us to do. That is the purpose of Revelation. It's not a book that hides truth from all but a gifted few. To the contrary, it is about giving information so that all of God's family can know His plan.

What a blessing it is to know that God cares so much about all of His family that He left a plan that should leave no one in the dark when it comes to finding out what He has in store. We can take comfort today in knowing that our God is behind us and with us all the way. He is watching out for us and is willing to inform us of all that really matters in our lives.

Real Significance

He made it known by sending his angel to his servant, John... (1:1b)

There is quite a difference of opinion as to who the "John" of this book really was. Some say that he was the beloved apostle of Jesus and others say he was not. To fuss over his identity, however, is to miss the point of the writing. It is not the receiver of the message that is important; it is the One who sends the message that we need to concentrate on. The Father has put His plan for mankind into the hands of the Son, and the Son then reveals the Father's heart to His creation.

Too many times Christians major on the minors and miss the big picture. The angel is the messenger and John is the conduit to pass the message on to the Church. They are just minor role players in the huge drama that is about to unfold before their eyes. The true focus here is back on the Son, who is worthy to be praised for what He is about to share with His coheirs. It's *His* angel and *His* servant. He is in charge and He is about to use His chosen instruments to share His story with the rest of creation.

We who serve the King of all kings are the most blessed of the earth. We may sometimes think that we are insignificant, but God cares about us all. He cares enough to provide a plan for our world that He is willing to share with finite beings. Certainly the angel and John have starring roles in this revealed drama, but the Writer, Director, and Producer of the universe is blessing us as members of the audience to this great story that is about to begin.

Do you feel insignificant? You are not! There is no one who is higher in life than the one who serves and abides at the foot of the cross.

Truth-And Nothing But the Truth

*He made it known by sending his angel to his servant
John, who testifies to everything he saw - that is, the word
of God and the testimony of Jesus Christ. (1:2)*

Whoever this "John" was, he was no doubt chosen because of his faithfulness to report the facts as they are presented to him. He was careful not to add to or take away anything from the message that is being revealed to him. There is a time and place for embellishment, but this certainly is neither.

What a lesson and warning for all who have the responsibility of sharing the Word of God with Sunday School classes, congregations, and students of the Bible. It is not the job of the messenger to alter the story or change the original meaning to fit a more contemporary setting. Just as the Apostle Paul admonished Timothy, we are to do our "best to show ourselves approved, a workman who does not need to be ashamed and who *correctly* handles the word of truth" (II Timothy 2:15, italics mine). John obviously realized the importance of the message and the source from which it came.

There is an old television margarine commercial that used the line, "It's not nice to fool Mother Nature!" Of even more importance is the seriousness of the message that is presented in the Revelation. When Bible teachers take this message out of its original context and try to make it fit current events they do a terrible injustice to the integrity of the Word and the faith that we hold so dear. Two lines given to me by former Bible teachers are: 1) "A text out of context is nothing but a pretext," and 2) "The Bible can never say what the Bible never said." These are good rules to keep in mind whenever we investigate any part of the Word of God. Mother Nature is not the only one that it is not nice to fool!

A Serious Blessing

Blessed is the one who reads the words of this prophecy, and blessed are those who hear it and take to heart what is written in it, because the time is near. (1:3)

There is a three-fold blessing in these words that have been noted by Bible students for centuries. Blessed are the people who read the words, hear the words, and those who will take to heart the words recorded here. Anyone who has literary skills can read the words and anyone who has a sense of hearing can listen to what is being read. However, the full blessing only comes when the third part of the beatitude is realized. It is those who take the meaning of the words seriously and structure their lives in accordance with them who can get in on the rewards that come from the blessing.

As with the entire Bible, the words of the Revelation are meant for our edification and benefit. They are not meant to be a sermon that we will hear and forget. The reading is not to be "checked off" as one more spiritual exercise completed. These are words for us to ponder, to chew on, and to let sink in. God has been gracious enough to provide for us an open door to see what He has planned for this world and to take this opportunity lightly would be foolish indeed.

John gives us the reason for the seriousness with which we should approach these writings: "The time is near." Though centuries have passed since these words were originally penned, the urgency has not passed. The time for fulfillment is closer now than ever. We dare not be asleep at our posts in these last days. Great events are happening all around us and we want to be wide-awake to see just what the Lord has in store for us and for our world.

The One and Only

John, to the seven churches in the province of Asia: Grace and peace to you from him who is, and who was, and who is to come, and from the seven spirits before his throne, and from Jesus Christ, who is the faithful witness, the firstborn from the dead, and the ruler of the kings of the earth. (1:4-5a)

What a great blessing it is to receive a proclamation of grace and peace from the One who rules heaven itself! It is a bestowment of love and inner tranquility that can only come from God. This is more than a blessing from an earthly friend. It is a pronouncement that God is providing power for whatever we need today.

There is a specific address here to the seven churches in Asia that John has in mind as he writes. In doing so, he gives a threefold greeting giving us a glimpse of the Holy Trinity, namely, the Father, Holy Spirit, and Son. The reference to the Holy Spirit, "the seven spirits before His throne" is most likely another way of describing the sevenfold ministry of the Holy Spirit as listed in Isaiah 11:2 (i.e., the Spirit: of the Lord, of wisdom, of understanding, of counsel, of power, of knowledge, and of the fear of the Lord).

Emperor worship was particularly popular in Asia in the first century, so John reminds the churches that in back of all human political activity stands the eternal Father, the Spirit of infinite wisdom, and the Christ, who is the ultimate ruler. No matter who is on the earthly throne, whether a king, a president, or a dictator, there is a power that is far above any type of government that man can conceive. The One who died on the cross and was raised from the dead is with us no matter what the world can throw at us today.

The Highest Calling of All

To him who loves us and has freed us from our sins by his blood, and has made us to be a kingdom and priests to serve his God and Father - to him be glory and power for ever and ever! Amen. (1:6b)

This verse is a reminder of all that Christ has done for us. We are not saved to continue to live in our sins, for the grace to be free from the power of sin has been made possible by the sacrifice on the cross. We don't have to be bound in a sin cycle, sinning continually, for we, as Christians, have been liberated and set on a path of holiness by the Master Himself.

In freeing us Christ has caused His body, the Church, to be His kingdom. We are more than just subjects, however, for we are also the priests that have direct access to the Father. We, the redeemed here on earth, are created to serve the Father just as all of heaven has also been created for His pleasure.

There are many metaphors used in the Bible for the relationship Christ has with His Church. We are called His body, His bride, His friends, and coheirs with Him. None, however, is any more precious than this idea of being priests. As priests we not only have direct access to God but also the privileges of sacrifice and burden bearing. A priest doesn't just officiate on holy days. A true priest intercedes for others continually. Just as Jesus is our high priest (Hebrews 4:14) and goes to the Father on our behalf as believers, we have a responsibility to lift those who don't know the way of salvation to the throne of grace. It's our calling and job! We may not always get paid according to what this world considers pay, but we will never be out of a job. As long as there are people and as long as there is time we are called by the Master to be His priests.

Let us also never forget that someone was Christ's priest for us, too.

The Not So Blessed Mourners

*Look, he is coming with the clouds, and every eye will see him,
even those who pierced him; and all the peoples of the earth
will mourn because of him. So shall it be! Amen. (1:7)*

One of the great truths that we as Christians hold dear is the belief that Jesus is coming again. There have been many who have scoffed at the idea and many charlatans who have deceived the gullible into believing their "date-setting" agendas as to when Christ's coming will occur. Still, it is one of the foundational tenets of our faith that Acts 1:11 will be literally fulfilled: "This same Jesus, who has been taken from you into heaven, will come back in the same way you have seen him go into heaven."

We certainly don't know the details about His return, but that is where faith comes in. We believe it will happen because the Bible says it. We believe it will happen, because without His return for us we have no hope. We believe it will happen, because deep within our hearts the Spirit witnesses to us and we know it is true.

We are also told here that all the people of the earth will mourn when He returns. That's not us. We are priests of the kingdom, for we were just told that in the previous verse. All those who are tied to this world's policies and priorities will certainly mourn, for they will realize too late just who is really in control of things. People can ignore, belittle, criticize, and twist the things of Christ now, but there is coming a day—a day when the King will return—when the scales will be balanced and truth will reign. People who belong to this world, not the eternal one, have a reason to mourn. However, for those of us who belong to the Kingdom of God, our party is just beginning!

The First and the Last

I am the Alpha and the Omega, says the Lord God, "who is, and who was, and who is to come, the Almighty. (1:8)

Alpha and Omega! They are simple words; they are profound words. They are, of course, Greek words. They are the first and last letters of the Greek alphabet. In a normal context they would just be like any other letters, but in this context they are a description of God.

It means that before there was anything else, there was God. It means that after everything else is over, there will be God. We may think that we have a handle on our lives and can maintain a degree of control over what our fates will be, but if we do we are just fooling ourselves. Our Creator will not give up His throne to anyone.

We don't like to feel weak. We don't like to be small. We don't like to admit that there are things that we can't figure out. In fact, some are arrogant enough to think that they have even figured God out. However, John tells us very clearly that there is just one *Almighty*.

It's good therapy for us to learn to be subservient and submissive. The Prophet Isaiah foreshadowed what John is saying when he penned these bold words, "I am the Lord; that is my name! I will not give my glory to another or my praise to idols" (Isaiah 42:8). There is no god like our God and no king like our King. That's basically what John was trying to say.

So today as we go about our business, let us keep in mind that we are not in charge; we are not our own masters. The Lord God is king. He always has been and always will be—regardless of what anyone else says.

Suffering

I, John, your brother and companion in the suffering and kingdom and patient endurance that are ours in Jesus, was on the island of Patmos because of the word of God and the testimony of Jesus. (1:9)

There are those who would say that being a Christian means that the struggle is over and God will provide a path of health and wealth for all who believe in His name. That's not what the Bible teaches, however, and certainly not something John would agree with. He was in exile—most likely sent to die—because of his faith in and stand for Jesus Christ. He was learning patience and endurance. He was experiencing suffering. He was finding out just how great a price there is that must be paid to follow Jesus.

I have witnessed saints who have gone through terrible diseases and suffering but still had a testimony on their lips. There have been brothers and sisters in the faith who have experienced brutal deaths and bodily humiliations just for the cause of Christ. Throughout the Christian era, millions have suffered hardships and deprivation to be counted among the host of believers.

This world of ours will never understand why it is that Christians are willing to go through such trials when they could renounce their faith and escape the suffering. We who truly are in Christ know why, however. We have tasted of the heavenly manna, and it is so sweet that we will not lose it for anything.

So if today you are tested and experience suffering for your faith, remember what good company you are in. Suffering does not mean that God has forsaken us; in fact, it may just be the preparation we need to be ready for the next assignment that is coming our way. The Christian way has always been the way of the cross. It's time that we carried our share of the load.

Being "in the Spirit"

On the Lord's Day I was in the Spirit, and I heard behind me a loud voice like a trumpet, which said: "Write on a scroll what you see and send it to the seven churches: to Ephesus, Smyrna, Pergamum, Thyatira, Sardis, Philadelphia and Laodicea. (1:10-11)

There is something very significant about the fact that John was "in the Spirit" on the Lord's Day. Since very early in the history of the Church, the first day of the week was set aside as a day to honor the resurrection of Christ. Early Christian Jews would keep the Sabbath (Saturday) and worship on Sunday as well. As the Church became more Gentile in membership, the Jewish Sabbath was dropped and the celebration of Christ's resurrection took center stage.

Being "in the Spirit" does not necessarily mean that John was in a trance or some ecstatic state on that Sunday. It means that he was in tune with the Spirit of God and was worshipping. Worship didn't require him to have other believers, a hymnbook, pews, an altar, or even a Bible. All that was necessary was a heart full of love for his Lord and making time for focused praise.

So often in our modern world Christians rush to get ready for church and then rush off to sit in a pew so someone else can try to pump them up for worship. This was not the case with John. No one had to get him ready. He was "in the Spirit" and longed for closer communion with his Master.

Perhaps that is why Jesus had a message for him to pass along to others. Maybe the source of his being able to encourage others wasn't just his suffering, but his being "in the Spirit." Maybe if we also spend more time "in the Spirit" we, too, will have a word from the Lord that will bring insight to a world needing to hear from God. Why not try a little preparation for worship this Sunday and see?

The Beginning of Symbols

I turned around to see the voice that was speaking to me. And when I turned I saw seven golden lampstands, and among the lampstands was someone "like a son of man," dressed in a robe reaching down to his feet and with a golden sash around his chest. (1:12-13)

We find later on that the seven lampstands are the seven churches that John is to address and that Jesus is the one who stands among them. What a beautiful picture. Jesus, the Lord of all, is standing in the midst of His churches. This should be a comforting thought to every pastor and faithful laborer in the Kingdom.

Christ is described as wearing a robe with a golden sash. The robe is the symbol of the Old Testament priesthood and the Jewish high priest wore the golden sash. Here Jesus is depicted as the high priest of His Church with all the authority and power that go along with that position.

This is the first of many images and symbols that are to come in this book. We must understand that this Revelation is written in code, but the key to the code is the Old Testament. John is not looking forward to tell us of the plan of God. He is looking backward to things he is very familiar with to give the first century Church insights into the heart, mind, and plan of God. If we want to unravel the mysteries of this book we, too, must look back into the sacred pages of the Old Testament, not to scenes and events that are in the present. John didn't know about the twenty-first century, but he did know Jewish history and about the first century. If we want to understand his message we must use the same method of interpretation that he intended his original readers to use. Otherwise, all we will get out of this book will be twisted and confused.

Maturity at Its Finest

His head and hair were white like wool, as white as snow, and his eyes were like blazing fire. His feet were like bronze glowing in a furnace, and his voice was like the sound of rushing waters. (1:14-15)

In the United States maturity has fallen on hard times. When one gets old he or she is generally considered less important than those who are young. If you doubt this, just notice the number of local church ministries for the young as compared to those provided for the elderly.

However, in many parts of the world—and certainly in John's world and in his time—age is revered. That's what John means as he describes the Ancient of Days. The white head and hair signify maturity, wisdom, and knowledge, for time doesn't weaken the eternal; it only magnifies His greatness.

The blazing eyes are the penetrations of His Spirit into our very beings. He knows all and sees all. The bronze feet represent strength and stability while the thundering voice proclaims words that cannot be ignored. John is painting a verbal picture of the attributes of Christ.

We so often see in our minds what artists have depicted Christ to look like. We may see Him with a beard, long hair, a square jaw, and strong, masculine features. Usually, we see Him looking a lot as we would like Him to look. What John does is show who Christ is, not what He looks like. He is wisdom, knowledge, omniscience, and power. He is Lord and we are His subjects. He is worthy of all honor and praise. There is no one like Him and no painting would ever do Him justice. As John stood amazed in His presence, so should we, for the Son of God is with us still.

The Messenger of the Message

In his right hand he held seven stars, and out of his mouth came a sharp double-edged sword. His face was like the sun shining in all its brilliance. (1:16)

Verse 20 will give us the interpretation about the identity of the stars. They are the "angels" of the seven churches that John is about to address. We may call them "leaders," or "pastors," but it is clear that they are the ones responsible for the welfare of their congregations. Christ has a message for each of them and that is what this book is all about. The Master who walks among the churches and holds their shepherds in the palm of His hand is about to speak. It would be wise for each church and each leader to pay attention to what He is about to say. We need to pay attention as well, for the messages given to the churches then are still applicable to the churches now.

We read of a "sharp double-edged sword." The words of Jesus will cut away all the stuff that doesn't matter and get right to the core issues that are affecting the lives of people in His Church. He never beats around the bush. The sword of His mouth will cut out what is hurting, and as the divine scalpel He will surgically improve our ability to function to the glory of the Father.

The countenance of the Lord is amazing. To be in His presence is like staring into the noonday sun, for He drives away all shadows and leaves everything open to His penetrating gaze. John is no doubt overwhelmed by what he experiences as he worships "in the Spirit" (vs. 10).

This is a good reminder that Christ is still Lord of His Church. He, the epitome of mercy, compassion, and power, never lets those attributes out of His grasp.

Keeping the Relationship Sacred

When I saw him, I fell at his feet as though dead. Then he placed his right hand on me and said: "Do not be afraid. I am the First and the Last. I am the Living One; I was dead, and behold I am alive for ever and ever! And I hold the keys of death and Hades." (1:17-18)

Isn't it amazing that so many people hear from God these days? People talk about hearing God tell them things, about getting visions, and about having dreams of major significance. Often they tell of these supernatural encounters in the same manner that they describe picking up their dry cleaning.

When John saw Christ he was awestruck. Actually, that's the reaction of every person I can think of in scripture. It was true for Abram, for Samuel, for Manoah, for Daniel, for Mary, for Peter, and for Paul. In fact, the presence of the Almighty is so frightful that the first words to the human being spoken that encounters the divine are always, "Do not be afraid."

As Christ speaks to John He recites His credentials. "First and Last…Living One…alive forever…holding the keys of death and Hades." This is no ordinary encounter. This is a face-to-face meeting with the Son of God. There has never been anyone like Him and there will never be anyone like Him.

As we contemplate our relationship with Christ, though we realize that He is closer than a brother to us, we must also never forget who He is. He is more than our "buddy." He is our Savior, Lord, and King. We dare not become too casual with Him. We must always honor Him as the Almighty One He is. He deserves our praise, adoration, and utmost respect. Let us never take Him off His holy pedestal. We can never give Him too much glory and praise, and we can never exalt Him beyond what He deserves.

Stepping into the Mysterious

Write, therefore, what you have seen, what is now and what will take place later. The mystery of the seven stars that you saw in my right hand and of the seven golden lampstands is this: The seven stars are the angels of the seven churches, and the seven lampstands are the seven churches. (1:19-20)

We have seen these words before. Christ is holding His pastors in His hand, and He walks among the churches. That should bring us comfort, but it should also cause us to wake up.

If Jesus told His disciples anything He told them to watch and be ready. He warned about the seven foolish virgins (Matthew 25), the unfaithful rich man (Luke 12), and the unjust steward (Matthew 16). He repeatedly reminded those who followed Him that they needed to work while it was day for the night was coming when no man could work. He reminds the Church that He is its companion and source of strength, but in the following verses we are going to see that He is also its judge.

There is no past or future for those in eternity. There is only the present. Time is a man-made tool for measurement, but without the boundaries of seconds, hours, days, months, weeks, years, and centuries, time loses its meaning. When John is told to write down what he sees and is about to see, it is for the benefit of us mortals. This doesn't mean that what John sees is way out there in the future. It just means that he hasn't seen it yet—but he is about to.

As we venture into the following chapters let us be aware of the "present" of the presence of God. The message to come is not for the future, for it is timeless. It is for us right now, regardless of what generation we live in.

Never Out of His Sight

To the angel of the church in Ephesus write: These are the words of him who holds the seven stars in his right hand and walks among the seven golden lampstands. I know your deeds, your hard work and your perseverance. I know that you cannot tolerate wicked men, that you have tested those who claim to be apostles but are not, and have found them false. You have persevered and have endured hardships for my name, and have not grown weary. (2:1-3)

One theme that these letters will repeat over and over are the words, "I know." Christ knows what is going on wherever His Church is located and all about the conditions that surround it. That should bring us comfort. Jesus knows about how hard and steadfastly we work. He knows how faithful we try to be. He knows about the hardships we go through for His sake. Our Lord is not ignorant as to our need; He knows!

This is a New Testament passage recapturing the idea of Psalm 139. No matter where we go, we can't escape His presence or His steadfast love for us. Just as the Ephesian church could rely on the continual fact of Christ's Spirit among them, we can be assured of the same grace in our lives.

Perhaps this would be a good place to just stop and give praise and thanks to God for His constant watch care over us. More than we care for our own children, He cares for His. More than we could ever appreciate what our children go through, He provides insights into the lives of us, His children, which reach to our very cores of existence. There is no way to describe His love for us because He is the essence of love, and His presence defies all definitions. As has been said, "God is good—all the time!"

"Give thanks to the Lord, for he is good; his loves endures forever" (Psalm 106:1).

Called to Love

Yet I hold this against you: You have forsaken your first love. Remember the height from which you have fallen! Repent and do the things you did at first. If you do not repent, I will come to you and remove your lampstand from it place. But you have this in your favor: You hate the practices of the Nicolaitans, which I also hate. (2:4-6)

The other shoe finally drops on the church. Though it has many admirable points, the Lord is not pleased with its members. In their zeal to be thorough and theologically correct, they left behind the love that made the church different from the world. The prescription is very clear: "Remember... Repent...Redo." The church at Ephesus needed to get a good look at itself and get its priorities back in order.

This message is so powerful for the Church of today. Because there is so much "folk theology" filtering in among the pews and sometimes downright heresy that passes as Christian doctrine, it is easy to want to keep the church clean and put the wrongdoers in their place. However, the mission and message of the Church is always to be one of love. Even when Jesus commends the Ephesians for hating the practices of the Nicolaitans, He never tells them to hate the Nicolaitans. He tells them to hate their practices.

The world doesn't always understand how Christians can hate the sin yet love the sinner. Often we are branded with terms such as "bigots," "hate-mongers," and "gay bashers." If we show anything but love for the person who sins, we are guilty of the charges against us. But if we hate the sin and love the sinner, then we are walking in the same path that Jesus did. That is what we are called to do, and Christ will never be pleased with anything less from His followers.

Love and Correction

He who has an ear, let him hear what the Spirit says to the churches. To him who overcomes, I will give the right to eat from the tree of life, which is in the paradise of God. (2:7)

The refrain, or chorus, which is contained in all the letters, is given here, and there is also a promise connected to it. If the church will overcome this problem of their lost love, they will eat of the tree of life—that is, to enjoy all the life that the world to come has in store for redeemed humanity. This can only be understood by recalling the story of the Garden of Eden (Genesis 2–3). The final verse of chapter three records that after man's disobedience and expulsion had taken place, the angel with the flaming sword stood at the east of the garden to bar the way to the tree of life. But in Christ, the paradise is restored and the way to the tree of life is opened. "Blessed are those who wash their robes, that they may have the right to the tree of life" (Revelation 22:14). It's a promise of eternal life for the redeemed.

Isn't that just like our Lord? He doesn't bash the church at Ephesus for their misdeeds but gently rebukes them to get them back on the right track. He is not happy with the way they have been doing ministry, but they still belong to Him and He loves them dearly.

All of us at times need a little correction to keep us going the right way. In fact, Hebrews 12:10 tells us "God disciplines us for our good, that we may share in his holiness." We need to hear the truth, and that is exactly what the Master provides for His Church. We are overcomers only through Him.

Alive Forevermore

To the angel of the church in Smyrna write: These are the words of him who is the First and the Last, who died and came to life again. (2:8)

There are many facets of theology in the Christian faith. Christians sometimes go to great lengths just to bicker about them. When it comes to the study of Revelation, people of faith are all over the place. Just listen to the list of ideas: postmillennialism, premillennialism, amillennialism, pretribulation, midtribulation, posttribulation, rapture, dispensationalism, preterist views, futurist views, centrist views, and the list goes on and on and on. Before you finish reading this book, there will probably be several ideas with which you take issue.

The one thing on which we can all agree, however, is the fact that Jesus died and came to life again. The story of the cross and resurrection is not negotiable. If we are in Christ and Christ is in us, then we believe in the resurrection. Perhaps the Apostle Paul said it best in I Corinthians 15:19: "If only for this life we have hope in Christ, we are to be pitied more than all men." The Church was built and survives on the truth that Christ was raised from the dead and that we who trust in Him will also be raised to life everlasting.

This truly is "Good News!" The One who is before all and will be around after all is said and done is the One who promises us the life that He now has. The resurrection is not a myth. It is not an idle dream for those who don't have much in this world, so they might as well hope for the next. The resurrection is fact and we have a risen Savior to prove it. As the old song says, "He lives! He lives! Salvation to impart! You ask me how I know he lives; he lives within my heart."

True Riches

I know your afflictions and your poverty - yet you are rich! I know the slander of those who say they are Jews and are not, but are a synagogue of Satan. (2:9)

Do you ever wonder who is keeping score? Does it sometimes seem as if the harder you work to get ahead the more ground someone else gains? Is it really possible that Christ could mean that those in destitute condition are really rich?

Because I have had the opportunity to travel not only throughout the United States but also to various parts of the developing world, I have seen mankind in all stages of wealth and poverty. I have witnessed some who have no homes at all and some who live in cardboard shacks. I have also been in some palatial estates that literally reek of money and status. It is so true that we, as humans, are far apart when it comes to equality in material wealth.

That's not what Jesus was talking about, though. The church in Smyrna had nothing that this world could call wealth, and they were being greatly mistreated for their faith. However, Christ found immeasurable wealth within them. Though they were slandered and libeled and suffered great injustices from without, inwardly they were shining like gold. They belonged to the King, and all His wealth was theirs.

We should be encouraged. Suffering is not a sign of God's displeasure. Often it is the crucible that refines us to be like Him. It may be that we need to go through suffering not only to better refine our own experience in the Lord, but also to prepare ourselves to be of service to others for the cause of Christ. We can trust our Lord to be with us to the very end. Our Master was acquainted with suffering, and as He was we should be proud to be.

The Blessed Sufferers

Do not be afraid of what you are about to suffer. I tell you, the devil will put some of you in prison to test you, and you will suffer persecution for ten days. Be faithful, even to the point of death, and I will give you the crown of life. (2:10)

Those who preach a health-and-wealth gospel apparently never got this far in their reading of the Bible. In fact, they must have overlooked a great deal of the scriptures, for there is much in God's Word, both Old and New Testaments, about suffering. God's people have always suffered. Many have been poor, destitute, sick, and persecuted. To say that it is God's plan for us that we who trust in Him should always be wealthy, healthy, happy, and satisfied is just a complete corruption and misreading of the Bible. Check Hebrews 11:36–40 if you have any question about this.

Those in the church at Smyrna were going through terrible persecution, and it wasn't for being bad. Unlike other letters listed here, there is no condemnation of the church in any way. The Word of the Lord is one of encouragement, not criticism. They were suffering for doing well and they were going to go through pain, prison, persecution, and death before they would receive their reward.

The call to them and to us is to be faithful. Regardless of our circumstances, faithfulness is what God honors. When we are going through the fire it is not always easy to see the reason for our suffering, but we must remember that the Lord knows our situations and our hearts. He will reward us in due time if we do not shrink from the task He has placed before us or the place He has put us in to do it. We may be put to the test, but tests are to prove what we know. The one thing we know is that we in Christ will never be alone in the fire.

Hope

He who has an ear, let him hear what the Spirit says to the churches. He who overcomes will not be hurt at all by the second death. (2:11)

Most people don't like to think about death. For many it is a morbid subject that they can barely acknowledge exists. I have met some people who won't even talk about preparing a will, because they don't want to think about dying. Others take comfort in knowing there is a life after this life, but they still don't want to think about the process that is required to get there.

We as Christians need to get beyond these earthly fears. These words are words of encouragement. They were written to a church that was going through terrible times of persecution, and the end result would be that their lives would most likely be terminated—and probably not in the way we would like our lives to end. Still, there is hope here. Christians will pass through the passage of death just like everyone else, but they will only do it once. For those without Christ there is a second death, an eternal lake of fire (20:14) that is prepared for the enemies of the Kingdom of God. The Word is clear, "If anyone's name was not found written in the book of life, he was thrown into the lake of fire" (20:15).

Our verse for today, however, is about hope. Those who have been faithful to Christ have no reason to fear this eternal punishment. Death is just a passageway to life everlasting. Saints of God can live without fear of what is to come, because what is coming is only good. No matter in what age we live, we can be assured that to be in the presence of the Lord will make whatever trials we have to go through here more than worthwhile. The Lord has been preparing our place for 2,000 years. Certainly it is a future worth looking forward to.

When the Fire is Applied

To the angel of the church in Pergamum write: These are the words of him who has the sharp, double-edged sword. I know where you live–where Satan has his throne. Yet you remain true to my name. You did not renounce your faith in me, even in the days of Antipas, my faithful witness, who was put to death in your city– where Satan lives. (2:12-13)

How would you like to live in a city that is known to be the home of Satan? Not many towns would like to post on their city limits sign, "Welcome to Pergamum—Home of Satan, Prince of Evil!" We may feel that where we live has its share of problems and even sinfulness, but it looks as if Jesus is saying something more here.

Pergamum was a place where Christians died for their faith. According to church tradition, Antipas was the Christian pastor of the city, and he was killed by being placed inside a bronze calf and roasted alive. Not exactly the retirement plan that most of us have in mind. It wasn't easy to be a Christian there, and those who stood up for their faith usually paid for it with an untimely end.

Jesus never forgets what His servants go through for His sake, because He cares about each one of us and promises grace for the hour of testing. Remaining true to His name is a highly valued quality, and our Lord will not let our sacrifices go unnoticed or without reward.

We should remember, however, that it was our Lord that said, "No servant is greater than his master. If they persecuted me, they will persecute you also" (John 15:20). As we serve we should not expect a free ride, because Jesus didn't get one. Being a Christian always requires involvement with a cross, and there is just no way that a cross is going to be pleasant.

Talking the Talk and Walking the Walk

Nevertheless, I have a few things against you: You have people there who hold to the teaching of Balaam, who taught Balak to entice the Israelites to sin by eating food sacrificed to idols and by committing sexual immorality. (2:14)

The story of Balaam is told in Numbers 22–25. At first glance it appears that Balaam didn't come off too badly, because God caused him to bless the Israelites instead of cursing them as King Balak wanted him to. However, Numbers 25 opens by telling how the Israelites were drawn into sin by the Moabite women, apparently at the instigation of Balaam after the plan to curse Israel failed. He was later killed for his transgression (Numbers 31:8,16) and is spoken of as a warning throughout the Old and New Testaments.

There was more involved than just eating food that had previously been given to idols. Usually this meant joining in on the pagan practices, including the sexual immorality that went along with the eating. Though some Christians were paying for their faith with their lives, apparently other Christians in Pergamum were compromising their standards to save their skins and blend in with their wicked society. They didn't seem to realize that when a person goes along with the flow, that person usually goes down the drain.

This is a warning to us in our day as it is to Christians in every generation. We cannot give in to evil and still be pleasing to Jesus. There will always be opportunities to take shortcuts in our devotion, but the One with the blazing eyes will always see through our motives and judge accordingly. One thing we don't want to hear from Jesus is, "I have a few things against you." Whether today or at the end of our lives, those words would be the worst thing we could ever hear.

Freedom from Sin

Likewise you also have those who hold to the teaching of the Nicolaitans. Repent therefore! Otherwise, I will soon come to you and will fight against them with the sword of my mouth. (2:15-16)

The teaching of the Nicolaitans is the way of compromise or the opposite of the way of legalism. It is saying that because we have experienced and believed in the grace of our Lord Jesus Christ all things are now lawful for us. It is a doctrine that abuses grace just as legalism distorts it. In either case, the "Good News" turns sour and twisted.

This teaching has not died out over the centuries. To this day there are those who say that because they have put their faith in Christ, it doesn't matter how they live their lives. They can commit whatever sins they want with their bodies and minds because their heart and spirit is pure. It's the act of abusing grace.

People who think along this line need to listen to what Jesus has to say. His words are clear: "Repent…or…I will fight against them." It may be possible to fool some people with this warped theology, but our Lord is not deceived. Listen to the words of the Apostle Paul: "Shall we go on sinning so that grace may increase? By no means! We died to sin; how can we live in it any longer" (Romans 6:1–2).

Jesus did not die on the cross so that we could continue to live in sin but to free us from sin's grasp. Apparently there were some in Pergamum who misused and took advantage of God's grace. This is what has Jesus bringing down this condemnation. Let us today strive to live holy lives so that we will not only live in harmony with Christ ourselves, but also will not lead someone else down an illegitimate path.

Being an Overcomer

He who has an ear, let him hear what the Spirit says to the churches. To him who overcomes, I will give some of the hidden manna. I will also give him a white stone with a new name written on it, known only to him who receives it. (2:17)

The good news of the gospel always includes a way back for those who have gone astray. Anyone who will hear the words of the Spirit and heed them can start anew and enjoy sweet fellowship with the Lord Jesus Christ.

Here the church at Pergamum is promised, "hidden manna." Immediately our minds go back to the Israelites in the wilderness as God provided sustenance for the masses during their "wandering" time. We should also be reminded, however, of John 6:35 where Jesus says, "I am the bread of life. He who comes to me will never go hungry, and he who believes in me will never be thirsty." People often miss the tie between the words that John records from Jesus in his gospel and the promise here to the Church. Anyone who has the Spirit of Christ within can draw nourishment from Him eternally.

The Church is also promised a white stone with a new name on it. The stone is an ancient decree of innocence, and the new name is "Christian." Only those who know Christ can fully know the impact of belonging to Him. Being a Christian is like the old saying, "It's better felt than telt." This promise is for all who will overcome!

It doesn't take a special talent or skill to be an overcomer. It only takes ears that will hear and hearts that are willing to change. Jesus will take care of the rest. He has a prescription that will be just right to meet whatever needs we may have—today and forever.

Measuring Our Growth

To the angel of the church in Thyatira write: These are the words of the Son of God, whose eyes are like blazing fire and who feet are like burnished bronze. I know your deeds, your love and faith, your service and perseverance, and that you are doing more than you did at the first. (2:18-19)

From the King of kings who has the penetrating eyes and unconquerable strength come the familiar words, "I know," and He has comforting things to say to the church. They are making progress. They are doing more than they used to do in the areas of love, faith, service, and perseverance, and that's not a bad reputation for any church to have.

It's a good measuring stick for any congregation or any individual to use. How do we know if we are making progress in our Christian walk? How do we know if Christ is pleased with how we are living our lives? We can look at Christ's words of commendation to this church and then check to see if we measure up. Are we showing more love than we used to? Are we stronger in our faith than we used to be? Are we doing more for others than we used to do? Are we holding fast even when things are not going as smoothly as we would like?

This is what Christ looks at and the standard by which He evaluates our growth. We don't have to wonder whether we are doing well or are not spiritually because He gives us measurable qualities here. If we have any question about how we are doing, we can ask our church family or accountability group how we are doing in these areas. This is one reason why the body of Christ is so valuable and why Christians were never meant to make it on their own. It would certainly be better to find out now how we measure up than to stand before Christ someday and be found wanting.

That Woman Jezebel

Nevertheless, I have this against you: You tolerate that woman Jezebel, who calls herself a prophetess. By her teaching she misleads my servants into sexual immorality and the eating of food sacrificed to idols. (2:20)

This church has a problem. In the midst of the good things that are happening there is an outbreak of false doctrine that is diminishing the image of the Christ. The focus of the problem is a woman by the name of Jezebel, but she comes by many names and sometimes the problem person is not even a woman. The point that is being made for the Church today is that Christ will not tolerate sinful action within His body.

There are many congregations of all generations that have fallen into this trap. The Apostle Paul also describes this group as, "lovers of pleasure rather than lovers of God—having a form of godliness but denying its power" (II Timothy 3:5). It is the way of compromise and the way of worldliness. As Christians we must be ever vigilant against the temptation to become like the world, for it is the world we are trying to bring to salvation. We cannot adopt its practices and still be the Church that Christ has called us to be.

Obviously, these sins are very blatant, but sometimes they take a more subtle approach. We have been called to holiness, and there is no room for sexual misconduct or lowering of biblical standards in the way of the cross. The Christian way is to be like Christ, and He allows no compromises. Grace is sufficient to change the world, but grace that is abused carries its own penalty. Jezebel wouldn't listen or learn. The results of her disobedience will come as surely and fully as the Word of the Lord. We need not be counted among her followers of sin. Hopefully, we will be wiser than she was.

Sin–Always Against God

I have given her time to repent of her immorality, but she is unwilling. So I will cast her into a bed of suffering and I will make those who commit adultery with her suffer intensely, unless they repent of her ways. I will strike her children dead. Then all the churches will know that I am he who searches the hearts and minds, and I will repay each of you according to your deeds. (2:21-23)

Aren't you glad that God is fair! He doesn't make unreasonable demands of us, but instead gives us direction and plenty of time to carry out His instructions. His patience is nearly unbelievable. There does come a time, however, when He stops waiting for us to respond to His leading and then He takes action. Such is the case with some of the people in the church in Thyatira.

Jezebel had been warned of the consequences of her sin, but she wouldn't mend her ways. She would now pay the inevitable penalty for rebellion against the Almighty, and not only would she suffer, but all those who followed her leadership would pay the price as well.

We need to remember that all sin is ultimately against God, and sin always affects more people than the individual sinner. If we would be unfaithful, others will be impacted by the outcome of our rebellion. This is done so that others will see the benefits of serving God and the repercussions for going our own way.

The One who knows us inside and out knows how to bless or punish us in ways that are intended to pull us back to His side. We need to be wise enough to realize that our arms are pretty short when it comes to boxing with God.

If we have loving parents, we know that we would not want to do anything that would cause pain to them. The same is true with our heavenly Father. Sin hurts Him because sin is rebellion against Him. He deserves better than pain from us.

Holding On to What You Have

Now I say to the rest of you in Thyatira, to you who do not hold to her teaching and have not learned Satan's so-called deep secrets (I will not impose any other burden on you): Only hold on to what you have until I come (2:24-25).

One of the privileges we enjoy in the Lord is the freedom to be able to remain in good standing with the King of kinds regardless of what others around us do. Certainly we are called to be watchmen and witnesses of God's grace and God's judgment to our world, but ultimately everyone makes his or her own decision about eternity and where one chooses to spend it.

Here we see that though Christ is not pleased with Jezebel and her followers of false doctrine, He will not penalize the innocent with the guilty. After all, this place is where good things are happening, and that part of the congregation needs to be rewarded, not punished. The Lord is fair.

In most churches today there are people who genuinely follow the Lord with a clear conscience and a clean heart, but there are also people who are just playing the game and are more like the world than the Kingdom. It is not our place to play judge and decide who is in which camp. The One who "searches the hearts and minds" is completely capable of discerning between the sheep and the goats, and He will make the final call when the proper time comes. Our job is to be faithful and trust the Holy Spirit of God to help us keep growing in grace even if others around us refuse to do so. We are not measured against the neighbors but against the Lord. Because Jesus is the same always (Hebrews 13:8) we can trust Him to do the right thing and not be deceived by those who attempt to mask the truth. The scales will all be balanced in the end.

True Rewards

To him who overcomes and does my will to the end, I will give authority over the nations—"He will rule them with an iron scepter; he will dash them to pieces like pottery"—just as I have received authority from my Father. I will also give him the morning star. He who has an ear, let him hear what the Spirit is saying to the churches. (2:26-29)

There is always a promise for the faithful of God. We don't serve Him to get rewards, but there are always rewards for those who serve. Since all authority is His, He can dispense it to anyone He pleases and in any way He pleases. One of the unique things about the gospel is that the Christian life is a series of paradoxes. The humble are exalted, the strong are humbled, the helpless are enabled, and the dead are raised. The Father is in charge and He has delegated all authority to the Son, who in turn presents it to His followers to meet the needs and challenges of their lives.

Are you struggling? Jesus knows that. Are you in need of help? He is closer than a brother to aid us in our journey. Do we need added unction and grace for the mission He has laid out before us? The heavenly King can and will provide what we need just for the occasion.

Over the centuries people who don't understand have scoffed at the way Christians live their lives, many times in poverty and with great sacrifice. What they don't realize is that God always pays His bills. He has promised power to be overcomers as we trust in Him and that's exactly what we get. The message is clear: In the end, we win!

We have to understand that our reward may or may not be received, even in part, in this world. It may not be material at all, but it is real and it *is* for all who will walk in the way of the Master.

Dead or Alive

To the angel of the church in Sardis write: These are the words of him who holds the seven spirits of God and the seven stars. I know your deeds; you have a reputation of being alive, but you are dead. (3:1)

What incrimination! It's one thing to try to pull the wool over the eyes of one's peers, but it just doesn't work too well with Jesus. Being thought to be alive, but really dead—that could be the definition of many churches today.

There are times when the "death" comes from ignoring the voice of the Lord, and there are times when well-meaning people just miss the path. It would seem, however, that the main culprit today is trying to match the world's definition of success. Churches become concerned about numbers, money, image, and reputation far more than holiness, ministry, sacrifice, and prayer. There are times when laymen lead these wayward wanderings, but ultimately the blame falls upon the pastor.

This letter is written to "the angel of the church," or in our terms, to the pastor or leader of the church. It is the leader whom Jesus will hold responsible, just as He does with the church in Sardis. He will not be fooled no matter how many people attend the services, how big the offerings are, how much education and prestige the pastor and members have, or how wonderful the reputation of the church in the community. Christ knows the truth, and He has no part in a "dead" church.

Our churches today need to read these words carefully. Live churches look and act like Christ. Dead churches look and act like the world. It should be easy for us to decide who belongs to whom. Certainly the Lord will have no problem at all in making that call.

Time to Wake Up

Wake up! Strengthen what remains and is about to die, for I have not found your deeds complete in the sight of my God. Remember, therefore, what you have received and heard; obey it, and repent. But if you do not wake up, I will come like a thief, and you will not know at what time I will come to you. (3:2-3)

The good news for the church is that it is not too late to reform. Though people are inwardly dead, they can be revived. The way back for the folks at Sardis is the same way back for people today who drift off to sleep in their walk with Christ. They are to remember what the relationship they had was like and remember what they had heard about the gospel, then repent of their waywardness and walk in the new way of life in obedience. We must always remember "God did not send his Son into the world to condemn the world, but to save the world through him" (John 3: 17). God wants always to revive our churches, not bury them.

However, the word of the Lord is clear. If they don't turn from their crowd-pleasing ways and become the Church Christ demands that they be, He will come to them unexpectedly in judgment. The pages of church history are full of great congregations that have withered after the sinful deeds of its leaders were exposed. Jesus will not be fooled. He will reward the faithful and punish the sinful. We can count on that on the authority of the Word of God. The Apostle Paul reminds all who will hear, "Do not be deceived: God cannot be mocked. A man reaps what he sows" (Galatians 6:7). Those who are slacking can turn from their idle ways and cause their lifestyles and their faith to become unified or they can continue down the path of least resistance, which leads to idolatry. Christ warns, but whether we heed or not is up to us.

Keep on Keeping On

> *Yet you have a few people in Sardis who have not soiled their clothes. They will walk with me, dressed in white, for they are worthy. He who overcomes will, like them, be dressed in white. I will never erase his name from the book of life, but will acknowledge his name before my Father and his angels. He who has an ear, let him hear what the Spirit says to the churches. (3:4-6)*

Would you like to get a real boost for the day? How about hearing directly from the Lord that you are worthy! I can't imagine anything that would bring more joy to a child of God than to hear those wonderful words. I have always been fascinated by the words of the angel to Daniel, "you are highly esteemed" (Daniel 10:11) and by the words spoken to Mary, "Greetings, you who are highly favored! The Lord is with you" (Luke 1:28). To be favored by God…what could be better?

That's the word to the faithful in Sardis and the faithful in Christ today. We don't have to wonder if we walk with God, for we have fellowship with God. As those in Sardis, we can look forward to walking in heavenly places in heavenly garb and hearing our names read from the book of life. We who are in Christ can spend eternity in the presence of God Almighty.

This should be an encouragement to those who keep themselves pure while even others in the church get dirty. Those who choose to draw near to God will find that He will hold them tight in the palm of His hand. No one has the power to tear us away from His grip.

Worthy! What a wonderful word. It must have seemed like music to the ears of the church in Sardis. Let us all live in such a way as to hear it from the Lord Jesus someday. "Well done, good and faithful servant," will be the sweetest sound that anyone will ever hear.

The Open and Closed Door

To the angel of the church in Philadelphia write: These are the words of him who is holy and true, who holds the key of David. What he opens no one can shut; and what he shuts no one can open. (3:7)

The church in the city of brotherly love got an unexpected present—a blessing and commendation from its Lord! They must have been a small congregation and probably didn't feel much like they would ever be noticed by the world, but here they are, immortalized by the words of John.

Jesus is introduced as the one who holds the key of David. What he opens, no man can shut, and what He shuts, no man can open. Again we see the Old Testament mind of John at work. The saying comes from Isaiah 22:22, where Isaiah hears the voice of God speaking about King Hezekiah's faithful servant, Eliakim. He hears the Lord say of Eliakim, "I will place on his shoulder the key to the house of David; what he opens no one can shut, and what he shuts, no one can open." As John brings this Old Testament image into New Testament view, he is saying that Jesus alone has the authority to admit someone into the New Jerusalem, the new city of David. He is the new, only, and living way into the presence of God. Jesus had already declared in Revelation 1:18 that He held the keys of death and Hades. *Holding the keys* in John's mind is determining who is really in charge.

No doubt many a church leader across the centuries has felt that he or she was small and insignificant. However, the Lord knows each of us well and knows how to meet our needs. Just as His promises rang true for the church in Philadelphia back at the close of the first century, they ring true for the faithful followers of Christ in the twenty-first century as well.

A Little and Christ Equal a Lot

I know your deeds. See, I have placed before you an open door that no can shut. I know that you have a little strength, yet you have kept my word and have not denied my name. (3:8)

What Jesus is literally saying here is that He has put an open door before the church, a door that has been open and remains open. The idea of an open door was familiar to the Christians of the first century just as it is today. The term was used by the Apostle Paul (Acts 14:27; I Corinthians 16:9; II Corinthians 2:12; Colossians 4:3) and by Christians down through the centuries. It is because of this verse that the church in Philadelphia became the symbol of the great missionary enterprise of the body of Christ. Since William Carey, the father of modern missions, felt the power of this verse leading him in 1792, more has been done in missionary impact than in the previous 1,500 years. Jesus understands that the church to which John is writing is not large, but a little strength combined with faithfulness to an all-powerful Savior is more than a match for any obstacle that the enemy can put in the way. Apparently the little church had passed through a time of trial and had held true. Christ is giving them His promise as a reward.

Often the church is aware that it only has a little strength. Our congregations may be small, our offerings may seem smaller, and our influence the smallest of all. But a little strength with Christ as an ally is all that is needed. Likewise, in our own lives, as members of His Church, we can claim the promise of His presence and power. Christ plus anyone is a powerful majority. Our Lord has not left us alone, regardless of our circumstances. He will be there for us until the very end of the age (Matthew 28:20), and that's a promise we can take to the bank.

Being True Jews

I will make those who are of the synagogue of Satan, who claim to be Jews though they are not, but are liars - I will make them come and fall down at your feet and acknowledge that I have loved you. (3:9)

In this verse we find a reference made to those who say they are Jews but are not. We are reminded that it is not a person's nationality or race that Christ considers, but whether or not a person is faithful to Him. Since those who are Jews by birth rejected Christ and the plan of God, they no longer are the chosen people of God or are even true Jews. The chosen people, or true Jews, are those to whom Christ has given His Spirit. The Church is now heir to all the promises made to Abraham and Israel. The people who are merely Jews by birth Jesus calls, "the Synagogue of Satan," and "liars." This does not mean the nation of Israel is evil, nor does it mean that Christians should be anti-Semitic, but rather that we should pray that they would eventually see the error of their ways.

This is a hard concept for many to grasp. We have been raised in a folk theology that teaches a literal interpretation of scripture without regard to its context and historical setting. John is very clear here, however, as is the message of the Master. Those who are Jews only by nationality have no part in the Kingdom of God. The same is true for those who are church members by position only or through an inherited tradition. It is the Spirit of Christ within an individual that makes a person belong to God. "And if anyone does not have the Spirit of Christ, he does not belong to Christ" (Romans 8:9b). That means that we can't count on our parent's or grandparent's religion to put or keep us in good standing with God. Every person is the captain of his or her own soul and every person will give an account before God. No one gets a free pass.

He Won't Give Up On You

Since you have kept my command to endure patiently, I will also keep you from the hour of trial that is going to come upon the whole world to test those who live on the earth. (3:10)

God is not going to be outdone. Loyalty has its sure reward. Since the Church has been faithful to Christ, they are going to be kept safe from the terrible trials that lie just ahead. This is not to say that they will not go through the trials, however. The Greek word here for *"from"* is not *apo,* which means *"away from,"* but *ek,* which means, *"out of."* The promise does not mean that they will be saved from going through temptation, tribulation, and trial, but that they will be kept out of it, just as swimmers keeps their heads out of the water. The Church may go through it, but they will not be overcome by it. It is a promise that the Lord will see His Church through any period of testing. It doesn't matter whether the tests that come our way concern our health, our income, our families, our peer groups, or even our local congregations. Christ will protect those who belong to Him, and He will be a debtor to no man.

This certainly is good news for the church. Since the early days of its existence, it has gone through the fire and yet it has done more than maintain; it has increased. Christ rewards faithfulness. We also may not appear to be the victor in the battles of this life, but certainly in the life to come there will be no question who is on the winning side.

We don't need to watch for a future tribulation period that may or may not happen and wonder if we can withstand it or have to be taken away before it occurs. We can count on these promises to see us through whatever comes. We are overcomers through the Word of Christ!

Pillars and Overcomers

I am coming soon. Hold on to what you have, so that no one will take your crown. Him who overcomes I will make a pillar in the temple of my God. Never again will he leave it. I will write on him the name of my God, and in the name of the city of my God, the new Jerusalem, which is coming down out of heaven from my God; and I will also write on him my new name. He who has an ear, let him hear what the Spirit says to the churches. (3:11-13)

There is no word of condemnation to this church. Christ moves right from the words of complement and promise to the words of reward and exhortation. He begins by telling the church that He is coming quickly. He promises that the overcomers will be pillars in the temple of God. A pillar was, and is, a great and honored support. The church at Philadelphia would see strength and stability in the promise. The character of the glorified saints will be fixed forevermore.

We have always had pillars in our churches. They are the saints who attend services or pay their tithes or do the work of ministry even when others won't. They stand fast even when it is not the popular thing to do.

On the overcomers Christ would write three names: "the name of my God...the name of the city of my God...my new name." The Old Testament crops up again as the name of God, signifying His ownership, was placed on the Israelites (Numbers 6:24-27). The reference to the New Jerusalem (which is described in chapters 21 and 22) is mentioned as a foreshadowing of what is yet to come. It has been suggested that the new name of Christ is a symbol for the fuller glories of His person and character that will be revealed at His coming. In essence, this part of the verse is saying that those who remain faithful to Christ belong to God, are citizens of heaven, and will know Christ even as he knows them. It is a great future that the Christian has to look forward to.

Put Up or Shut Up

To the angel of the church in Laodicea write: These are the words of the Amen, the faithful and true witness, the ruler of God's creation. I know your deeds, that you are neither cold nor hot. I wish you were either one of the other! (3:14-15)

The One who sees all, testifies to all, and rules over all once again calls to provide correction for His Church. This passage concerning the church at Laodicea has become synonymous with the church that no one wants to belong to. They have neither a fiery passion for the things of Christ nor a cold indifference. They are just apathetic and useless. They are like the salt that has lost its saltiness or the lamp that has been put under a bowl. They are ineffective servants of the Lord.

I don't know of another place in scripture where our Lord wishes for something. Here He "wishes" more for the Laodicean church. Of course, this is not a literal rendering of the original word, but the point is that Jesus is not satisfied with the condition of this church. He will never be satisfied with any local church or denomination that is "all show and no go."

This church has succumbed to two of the most dangerous of all temptations—complacency and affluence. When we get satisfied with where we are, we neither move ahead nor back. We just exist. There is more danger in Christianity for churches and individuals than we often contemplate. The more we have, the more we will have to justify before the Lord. There is more than just a ten percent tithe involved here. What we do with the other ninety percent is just as important. When we get too comfortable and satisfied, Christ is not. We need to remember that.

The Curse of the Status Quo

So, because you are lukewarm - neither hot nor cold - I am about to spit you out of my mouth. You say, "I am rich; I have acquired wealth and do not need a thing." But you do not realize that you are wretched, pitiful, poor, blind, and naked. (3:16-17).

Rejected by Christ! What a terrible thing for any person to have to face. It's even more terrible when one considers that this is His church He is talking to. People are never successful spiritually when they straddle the fence, and Jesus is not going to let the church in Laodicea, or any church for that matter, get away with it.

The big problem here is that the church could not see itself as Christ saw it. The members of the Church saw themselves as completely adequate and even well to do in every area, but Christ saw them, as they truly were—sickening and grotesque. This is why each of us and every congregation need to do a checkup occasionally to see how we are doing spiritually. It's too easy to be deceived and convince ourselves that everything is okay when the reality is otherwise. We are dependent on the Spirit of God to guide us, teach us, and convict us. We are continually needy creatures in search of God's mercy. Let us never get too high and mighty to think otherwise, for if we do we may find our lot cast with the Laodiceans and end up scorned by Christ instead of being blessed by Him.

Lukewarmness! It is the bane of too many churches today and it makes Christ sick to His stomach. Only the Holy Spirit can light a fire within our congregations and cause us to burn for the glory of the Father. If our fire has gone out it is time to repent, refocus, and turn up the spiritual thermometer. Revival is not an option for the Church if it is to continue to exist—it is a life or death necessity.

A Divine Prescription

I counsel you to buy from me gold refined in the fire, so you can become rich; and white clothes to wear, so you can cover your shameful nakedness; and salve to put on your eyes, so you can see. Those whom I love I rebuke and discipline. So be earnest, and repent. (3:18-19)

It would be a terrible thing to go to a doctor and have him tell us about a problem with our health, but not tell us what to do about it. We need a prescription for a remedy as well as a diagnosis if we are to get better.

That's exactly what Jesus does for this church. Though He is greatly disappointed with their behavior and attitude, He loves them. He doesn't want them to continue on the path they are on, so He shows them the way back. Laodicea had been known for its medical center, its cloth production, and its wealth. Jesus now shows them that they need to quit relying on the physical assets they possess, but instead turn to Him for true wealth, robes of righteousness, and a healing balm.

Christ is not willing that any should perish, but that all should be saved. Even if we disappoint Him, He still wants the best for us. He may discipline us to bring us back to our senses and get our act together, but He does so out of love. Just as parents who love their children discipline them, so Christ always does what He does with our interest at heart. When the Lord's discipline comes to us we need to accept it in the spirit in which it is given and heed the direction in which Christ wants us to go.

We have been given counsel by the "Wonderful Counselor" (Isaiah 9:6). The Church would be wise to heed the advice given. He speaks to make us what we should be so that we can be a vessel He can use for His glory and our good.

Outside and Looking In

Here I am! I stand at the door and knock. If anyone hears my voice and opens the door, I will come in and eat with him, and he with me. **(3:20)**

This is one of the saddest verses in the Bible. It's right up there with Samson not knowing that the Lord had left him (Judges 16:20), or Hezekiah realizing that Judah's situation was like a woman in the midst of childbirth and having "…no strength to deliver" (II Kings 19:3), or Judas going out, "And it was night" (John 13:30).

Here is Christ, pleading for the privilege of coming back into His church. This verse is often used in the presentation of the gospel to unbelievers in an attempt to get them to open their heart's door and let Christ in. The reality here, however, is that Christ has been locked out of His own church. He is patiently waiting, in a sickened condition because of their waywardness, and is begging for the right to have fellowship with His own family.

How great is the love of our Lord to have such patience and such compassion for His own. He truly is the Good Shepherd. How many churches have forced Him out because of their bickering, their selfish carnality, and their attempts to be like the world? The message is clear to the church—Jesus wants back in! He died for the Church to make it holy and to claim it as His own. How can we turn down such an offer of fellowship? If we have forced Him out through our apathetic attitudes or our indulgent lifestyles, we need to repent of our sins and invite the King of the Church back into the midst of His Church. Instead of letting Him knock, we need to throw the door of our fellowship wide open for His entrance and scrutiny. Without Him no church has a reason to exist.

If We Could Only Hear

To him who overcomes, I will give the right to sit with me on my throne, just as I overcame and sat down with my Father on his throne. He who has an ear, let him hear what the Spirit says to the churches. (3:21-22)

As the section dealing with specific addresses to the churches comes to a close, we have a familiar challenge and a familiar promise. The church is challenged to be overcomers and promised a reward if they will do so.

This is another example of the unchanging Christ (Hebrews 13:8). He always calls each church to overcome the obstacles that the enemy puts before it, and each one that does so will be eternally rewarded. What the churches need are ears to hear what the Master is saying. Deafness seems to be a perpetual problem. It was true for the first century, and it is true for today. Spiritual deafness and hardness of heart seem to be related, and Christ is the only cure for either.

Perhaps this hearing problem is because of the world's siren song. So often the Church wants to be like the world to attract the world, but in the process of being world-like it ceases to be Christ-like. We must remember that Jesus promised that if we would lift Him up, He would draw men to Himself (John 3:14–15). The Church needs to listen more than it needs to talk. In fact, if it doesn't listen to what the Spirit is saying, it really has nothing to talk about.

These seven churches were real and their situations were real. However, they are also examples of all churches everywhere and the message for them is also the message for us. Christ calls His Church to be pure, faithful, and patient. He calls us to hold fast for in the end we will be victorious. That is the message in its simplest form for this entire book.

The First Vision: Revelation 4:1-5:14

There is a great praise party going on in heaven from eternity to eternity. This is the backdrop for everything else that will ever happen. We are to believe in and worship the One on the throne (God the Father) and believe in and worship the Lamb (God the Son).

Looking Through the Open Door

After this I looked, and there before me was a door standing open in heaven. And the voice I had first heard speaking to me like a trumpet said, "Come up here, and I will show you what must take place after this." (4:1)

Up to now all that we have been reading in this book has been merely a prelude. We now begin with the first vision. There will be six more after this one. One thing we are not given in this portion of scripture is a time line. We don't know how much time passed between chapter three and chapter four. All we know is that John takes us along with him in a heavenly vision. It would be nice to be able to ask him some questions along the way, but I guess we are going to have to wait on that.

The experience that John had in chapter one was similar to the one that Isaiah had (Isaiah 6:1-8), but this vision is also more like what happened to Ezekiel (See Ezekiel 3:14-15; 8:1-4 for more clarification). As we have seen so many times before in this study, the key to understanding Revelation is found in our understanding of the Old Testament, for John uses many allusions to it in his writing. Without the focus on what was available to the Christians of the first century to use in interpreting John's words, we will get lost in a wilderness of speculation. This is where the modern church has so often gone wrong in reading this book.

We must be very careful here to understand what this vision means. John is still writing to the seven churches, and this message must make sense for them as well as us. Scriptural context must be honored throughout this book if anyone is to profit from it. Growing in grace and growing in knowledge go hand in hand.

Life "In the Spirit"

At once I was in the Spirit, and there before me was a throne in heaven with someone sitting on it. And the one who sat there had the appearance of jasper and carnelian. A rainbow, resembling an emerald, encircled the throne. (4:2-3)

Being "in the Spirit" here means that John has entered a kind of daydream. A great vision is going to be shown to him, and he is "spiritually" taking the journey of a lifetime.

No description of the person on the throne is given. John could only say that looking at God was like looking at precious stones. One cannot describe God; he can only register his impressions. In fact, much of this book can be thought of as impressionistic art, in contrast to more traditional art. John often uses symbolism and anthropomorphism (making God in man's image), but not here. God cannot be described. John can only say what He is like.

This scene definitely has an Old Testament background. It tells of a meeting between man and God, with a number of created beings also in attendance. It is similar to visions in Isaiah and Ezekiel, with nature responding to God with lightning, voices, and thunder, as at the giving of the Ten Commandments on Mount Sinai.

What a great God we serve. He is beyond description and is far beyond our understanding. The wisest people in the history of the world could only speculate about Him, yet the humblest have been able to draw right up next to Him. Perhaps the best we can do is just bow and give praise. As we shall see in the coming verses, that's exactly what they do in heaven. We are about to enter the "eternal praise party!"

One at Last

Surrounding the throne were twenty-four other thrones, and seated on them were twenty-four elders. They were dressed in white and had crowns of gold on their heads. (4:4)

The twenty-four elders are representatives of mankind with whom God has worked to reveal Himself to the world—the twelve patriarchs (leaders of the old Israel) and the twelve apostles (leaders of the new Israel). John was able to see something around the throne of God that he had never seen on earth—the union of Judaism and Christianity. Both groups had been chosen by God to reveal His plan of redemption to the world, so both groups are seen as rulers on thrones with God in His kingdom. The fact that the elders are dressed in white and crowned with gold signifies that they are priests and kings in the heavenly realm.

This is one of the great promises and hopes that we have for the world to come. It is where the prayer of Jesus comes to pass "that they may be one as we are one" (John 17:22). Just imagine a place where love is supreme and that tribal, cultural, and ethnic differences are all set aside. Imagine a place where there are no political parties and no one going by denominational titles. That's what it is like in the presence of God. No wonder it is called, "heaven!" While we keep working for God's will to "be done on earth as it is in heaven" (Matthew 6:10) we have the assurance that when we see Christ face-to-face it will be a complete reality. When we reach the world beyond this world, we will see a different picture than we have ever imagined. Our minds cannot even grasp a place that is not fragmented by hatred and self-advancement. For the divided world that John lived in and for the world of prejudice and bigotry that we so often live in, this is indeed "Good News!" We will be one at last.

Our God is an Awesome God

From the throne came flashes of lightning, rumblings and peals of thunder. Before the throne, seven lamps were blazing. These are the seven spirits of God. (4:5)

The seven lamps of fire complete the picture of the seven lampstands, which were the seven churches (1:20). They are lighted with a light not their own, for the light of the Church is the Spirit of God. The seven Spirits are the work of the Holy Spirit manifested to and through the seven churches, which is the complete revelation of God to the world. We can assume that if all ten churches of Asia had been chosen, ten Spirits would have been named.

Here is a lesson that the Church must never forget. We, as Christians, have no light in ourselves. We can only be the light of the world as reflectors of the divine Spirit of God that has come to reside within us. Whether our congregations are large or small, our collective luminary ability cannot even produce the brightness of a spark. We are totally dependent on the presence of the Lord to create the fire that can destroy sin and cause us to shine like cities set on a hill.

This is also another reference to the Old Testament, where John is paraphrasing the words of the prophet in Isaiah 11:2. In essence, John is saying: *The Spirit is of the Lord; the Spirit is the source of wisdom; the Spirit is full of understanding; the Spirit is the divine counselor; the Spirit is endless power; the Spirit is the source of knowledge; and the Spirit is the fear of the Lord.*

No doubt John is seeing something that he has never experienced before, and it must be overwhelming. The scene is one of power, majesty, and authority. It's bigger than being at a fireworks display for the first time. God's in His heaven, and what an awesome God we serve.

The God Who is in the Middle of It All

Also before the throne there was what looked like a sea of glass, clear as crystal. In the center, around the throne, were four living creatures, and they were covered with eyes, in front and in back. The first living creature was like a lion, the second was like an ox, the third had a face like a man, the fourth was like a flying eagle (4:6-7),

The "sea of glass" has a parallel in I Kings 7:23, where in Solomon's temple there is a "molten sea." The crystal sea shows the separation of God from all creation. It emphasizes the majesty and holiness of God. John seems to be at a loss to describe it, as well as the location of the four living creatures. We must remember, however, that this is a vision, and we cannot expect objects, persons, and relationships to be listed in concrete terms.

The identity of these creatures is of less importance than what they represent. Together the creatures represent the all-seeing and all-knowing power of God. There is a definite connection between this scene and Ezekiel's vision of the wheels, which accompanied the four creatures and is recorded as revealing, "all four rims were full of eyes all around" (Ezekiel 1:18). Individually, they represent the power and authority that God has established over His creation. The lion stands for strength, the calf for sacrifice, the face of a man for intelligence, and the eagle for the high and lofty, ever-present being of God. The creatures are not seen as having individual identities but are seen as likenesses and representations of the One who is on the throne.

Rest assured that today we serve a God who sees all and knows all. This passage describes the present, not a future representation of God. We can count on the all-knowing, ever-present, and all-powerful God to be with us wherever we are—right in the here and now!

Worthy of Worship

Each of the four living creatures had six wings and was covered with eyes all around, even under his wings. Day and night they never stop saying: "Holy, holy, holy is the Lord God Almighty, who was, and is, and is to come." Whenever the living creatures give glory, honor and thanks to him who sits on the throne and who lives for ever and ever, the twenty-four elders fall down before him who sits on the throne, and worship him who lives for ever and ever. They lay their crowns before the throne and say: "You are worthy, our Lord and God, to receive glory and honor and power, for you created all things, and by your will they were created and have their being (4:8-11)."

The idea of God as Creator and Ruler is brought out by the hymns that the living creatures sing. Because the creatures are reflections of God's attributes, they never cease to bring Him glory. They speak of God's holiness and eternal existence. They speak of His worthiness and majesty. From the example of the living creatures, John begins to see that there is no way to approach God except through praise. God's entire created universe gives praise to Him continually, and while the living creatures reflect God, they are also an example of His creation. As they chant His praises, the twenty-four elders join in as they bow before the throne. It is a beautiful picture. Heaven is where all of God's creation including mankind joins together in praise continually to the King of kings. The throwing of the elders' crowns shows that God alone must reign supreme.

We, as children of the King, are also to be daily participants in the "Praise Party" of heaven! It is not just something that goes on "on the other side." Our lives are to continually be an offering of praise to God by how we live, what we say, and how we impact our world. What is going on in the heavenly realms is to be a reflection of what is going on here. It's not going to happen perfectly here, of course, but we should make it our business to praise God here as best we can.

The Heavenly Anticipation

Then I saw in the right hand of him who sat on the throne a scroll with writing on both sides and sealed with seven seals. And I saw a mighty angel proclaiming in a loud voice, "Who is worthy to break the seals and open the scroll?" But no one in heaven or on earth or under the earth could open the scroll or even look inside it (5:1-3).

John's vision continues to follow the pattern of the vision of Ezekiel in its general outline. Ezekiel saw "a book," which he was told to eat. John sees a book in the hand of God on His throne.

John notices that the scroll has writing on both front and back, and it was sealed with seven seals. The seals indicate the secrecy of the contents of the scroll. It is significant that the scroll rests "in the right hand of him who sat on the throne." God alone knows what is written on it. This illustrates the fact that God's ways can never be known to man except by divine revelation. The scroll contains man's destiny, and mankind cannot know what the future holds except as God allows it to be revealed.

The easiest identification of this scroll is that it contains the prophecy of the end events, including both the salvation of God's people and the judgment of the wicked. It is God's redemptive plan for the movement of human history, the overthrow of evil, and the gathering of a redeemed people to enjoy the blessings of God's rule.

John sees a powerful angel coming on the scene who is calling for someone to break the seals of the book and make its message known. The angel looks through all creation but cannot find anyone who is powerful enough and who has the authority to make the message of the scroll available. There is only One who is worthy, and we are about to meet Him.

Dry Those Tears

I wept and wept because no one was found who was worthy to open the scroll or look inside. Then one of the elders said to me, "Do not weep! See, the Lion of the tribe of Judah, the Root of David, has triumphed. He is able to open the scroll and its seven seals (5:4-5)."

When no one was found who was able to open the book, John breaks down and cries. He is not crying just because his curiosity will not be satisfied, but because he knows that only God has the answer for the terrible times that the Church is going through. The fact that John is crying tells us that he is not in a "zombielike" state, but is in possession of his natural faculties. This account is not merely the playback of a tape recording, but shows he is able to recall, think, and arrange the events of the vision.

John's tears are pushed aside as one of the twenty-four elders tells him to not be concerned, because there has been found a person with two titles who can solve the problem of the book. He is referring to the "Lion of the tribe of Judah," and the "Root of David." These are references to the Messiah, and both titles are applied to Jesus. He has already triumphed over all that Satan could throw at Him, and He alone is able to break the seals of the scroll and reveal its contents. This victory over Satan, accomplished by Christ's coming as a man to earth, is frequently alluded to in the New Testament gospel accounts (Matthew 12:29; Luke 10:18; John 12:31; 16:11). This victory is not only over Satan but also over that entire host of evil spiritual powers (Colossians 2:15). He is our King—and He is worthy! The scene is played out like a great heavenly drama and obviously this is being told for John's benefit and for ours. The King of the Kingdom is about to make His entrance, and what He does makes all the difference for us today.

Enter, the King

> *Then I saw a Lamb, looking as if it had been slain, standing in the center of the throne, encircled by the four living creatures and the elders. He had seven horns and seven eyes, which are the seven spirits of God sent out into all the earth (5:6).*

John sees Christ and describes Him in a very different way than we are accustomed to imagining Him. Many artists have tried to imagine what this Jew from Galilee could possibly have looked like, but few have ever shown Him as John does here as a slaughtered Lamb with seven horns and seven eyes. Here are the Old Testament ideas of a Messiah who would be strong enough to rule (the horns are symbol of strength), but also a Lamb who would be led to His death for us (Isaiah 53). Both concepts fit Jesus perfectly. The perfect presence of God (the seven spirits) fit the interpretation of the sevenfold eyes. The Spirit of Jesus was promised to those on earth (John 14:16-20) and is evidence of God's continued care. The ministry and mission of Jesus have a twofold role to fulfill. First, He must come in humility and meekness to suffer and die; then at the end of the age He must return in power and glory to put all His enemies under His feet. This is the interpretation of what John is seeing.

As we face new trials each day, we can be assured that there is a Redeemer who has paid the price for our sins and has invited us to participate in ultimate victory. We do not stand by as passive observers, for as Christ overcame we too can be overcomers today through His blood shed for us on Calvary. Like John, we are amazed at the grace that makes it all possible, but we should be eternally grateful that His sacrifice is beneficial for us still. Christ the Lamb is the King, and He has earned all that He receives. Certainly He is Lord of lords also!

Jesus - the Answer to Our Prayers

He came and took the scroll from the right hand of him who sat on the throne. And when he had taken it, the four living creatures and the twenty-four elders fell down before the Lamb. Each one had a harp and they were holding golden bowls full of incense, which are the prayers of the saints. (5:7-8)

John sees Jesus standing in the center of the throne (the very person and presence of God) and He takes the scroll from the Father. Christ now holds the center of attention and He has earned it. He has also earned the right to open the seals, which will bring to pass the revelation of, and the executing of, the plan of God for our sinful world. He has earned the right of authority because of His victory over sin, death, and the grave. This is the high point of John's vision. It reaches its peak as the Lamb steps forward and takes the book lying on the outstretched hand of God. In this brief picture the story of man's redemption is reenacted as Christ opens the seals of the book and goes out to bring to pass the will of the Father.

When Jesus takes the book, worship breaks out among the twenty-four elders and the four creatures. As they play their harps and take note of the prayers of the saints, they begin to sing. Christ is worthy of praise! He is the solution to humanity's problems. He is the one hope for the human race. He is the center of the Bible, the center of history, the center of Christian experience, and the Lord and Master of life.

When we present Jesus to the world, this is the image we need to show them. Without Him we have nothing and with Him we have everything. He truly is the answer to our prayers, and those prayers are kept before Him continually!

The New Song

And they sang a new song: "You are worthy to take the scroll and to open its seals, because you were slain, and with your blood you purchased men for God from every tribe and language and people and nation. You have made them to be a kingdom and priests to serve our God, and they will reign on the earth." (5:9-10)

The song they sing is a new one. It reflects the authority and majesty of Christ. It is new because the theme is new—Christ's divine merit. God's people have been redeemed and the Lamb is responsible for that and therefore is worthy of all praise. As the revelation of Christ and His Kingdom takes place at His second coming, His Church will fully exercise its royal priesthood. In the present instance, a new song is sung because the redeemed order of God's kingdom is about to be inaugurated. Revelation is characterized by new things: a new name for the redeemed (2:17; 3:12), the new Jerusalem (3:12; 21:2), a new song (5:9), new heavens and a new earth (21:1). All things are made new (21:5).

Newness of life is what we receive when we put our trust in Christ for our salvation. Our bodies get older each minute, and we all eventually will suffer the pains that come on with advancing age. But our relationship in Christ can be ever new. We don't have to let it get stale or our praise to be weak. This passage reminds us that right now in the presence of the throne of God a new song is being sung to celebrate our redemption. It's time that we cheer up and join the choir in worship of our Lord. We've got a lot to celebrate, and we are way behind in our praise.

New is not always good and it is not always bad. Songs can be meaningful or trite. This song is like no other for it reminds us that we have been bought with a price, and the price has been paid in full by the blood of the Lamb.

A Good Place For an Amen

Then I looked and heard the voice of many angels, numbering thousands upon thousands, and ten thousand times ten thousand. They encircled the throne and the living creatures and the elders. In a loud voice they sang: "Worthy is the Lamb, who was slain, to receive power and wealth and wisdom and strength and honor and glory and praise!" Then I heard every creature in heaven and on earth and under the earth and on the sea, and all that is in them, singing: "To him who sits on the throne and to the Lamb be praise and honor and glory and power, for ever and ever!" The four living creatures said, "Amen," and the elders fell down and worshiped. (5:11-14)

Added to the voices and praise of the twenty-four elders and the four living creatures is a chorus of thousands of angels. This great multitude circles all around the throne as they give praise.

Finally, all of creation in the land, sea, and air join in on the party of praise. The living creatures say "Amen" as the elders again fall down and worship. As representatives of creation in their endless worship of God, they conclude the worship service offered to God and the Lamb by the whole of creation from the beginning to the close of history.

The central thought of this vision in chapters four and five is made clear in this way. In chapter four we see the power of God the Creator; in chapter five we see the love of God the Redeemer. Chapter four says, "Believe in God"; chapter five says, "Believe also in me" (John 14:1). While believing in the power of God and the love of God, there is no enemy or force of evil that the church needs to fear. She can go into the conflict with the assurance of victory. The Almighty is still on His throne, which is above all thrones. Therefore chapters four and five are filled with songs of victory.

There is no reason for us to be downhearted today. We can put our trust in the Lamb knowing that He walks with us on every step of the path we take.

The Second Vision: Revelation 6:1-8:5

Throughout history there is the opening of the seals of the judgment of God.

1. **The first seal:** A spirit of rebellion (spirit of antichrist) will try to conquer the church continually from the first coming of Christ until the second (i.e.; the entire period of the last days). (6:1–2)
2. **The second seal:** War will be waged throughout the whole Christian era. (6:3–4)
3. **The third seal:** Famine will be the result of the conqueror that brings war to the face of the earth. (6:5–6)
4. **The fourth seal:** The natural outcome of the conqueror that brings war and famine is death. (6:7–8)
5. **The fifth seal:** Many Christians will be made martyrs as a result of the war waged against the Church, but after their death they enter into the eternal care of the Lord. (6:9–11).
6. **The sixth seal:** The focus shifts from God's judgment as a result of the acts of man to nature being used as God's tool of judgment. This brings us down to the end of time as rebellious men face the wrath of God. (6:12–17)
7. There is an interlude between the sixth and seventh seals. The people of God are sealed with His mark, and we return again to the heavenly praise party.
8. **The seventh seal:** This shows what is happening to the believers as a result of the first six seals. The entire people of

God are marked with His mark of ownership so that when the winds of trials and tribulation strike the earth, they will be eternally secure. As a result, they join in on the great praise party in heaven. (8:1–5)

Life is Not Just a Bowl of Cherries

I watched as the Lamb opened the first of the seven seals. Then I heard one of the four living creatures say in a voice like thunder, "Come!" I looked, and there before me was a white horse! Its rider held a bow, and he was given a crown, and he rode out as a conqueror bent on conquest. (6:1-2)

The first vision (chapters 4–5) serves as a prelude to what is to take place. John had previously written to the seven churches (chapters 2–3) with a word of exhortation, encouragement, admonition, and warning. They needed a promise of hope and help from the pressures that were gnawing at them from without and within. Like a spiritual pharmacist, John passes along the prescriptions from Jesus that will cure their ills.

The opening of the first seal reveals a white horse. The rider on the horse has a bow and a crown. It is easy to picture this rider as the Christ who is going into battle to win the victory for His saints. Though this is attractive to envision, a more accurate understanding is that the first horse and rider depict a conquering invader. The broken seals are showing calamities that will come on the earth. Since Jesus is the Lamb who is opening the seals of the scroll, it does not seem that He would be one of the characters on the scroll. Trying to put a name on this person or on a nation here is futile. The important thing to remember and understand is that John saw an invading conqueror as a judgment of God in the last days (i.e., the last days being from the first coming of Christ to the second coming of Christ). His message is that the Church of the Living God is going to be attacked. There may be some tough battles ahead. Physical death, however, has little consequence to those who have the seal of God (chapter 7). We have victory because Christ has already given us the victory.

A Time for War

When the Lamb opened the second seal, I heard the second living creature say, "Come!" Then another horse came out, a fiery red one. Its rider was given power to take peace from the earth and to make men slay each other. To him was given a large sword. (6:3-4)

The opening of the second seal brings about a red horse. Its task was to remove peace from the earth. Note that he was "given power." Nothing ever happens without being permitted by the King of all kings. The horse and rider represent the war that the first horse and rider will wage. This is the continuing conflict between the Church and the world. The color red symbolizes the tragedies of war. Mark 13:7–8 makes reference to the great war that is carried on down through the ages until Jesus returns.

We cannot blame God for the hardships and deprivations that war brings about. We blame sin, which causes selfishness and greed for power in the hearts of men. God has made a way to do away with sin through the blood of His Son, and whoever believes on Him completely is freed from the ravages of sin on the heart. As long as there is time, however, there will be men and women who resist the Spirit of God, and therefore the conflicts will continue. Many churches have put on their marquees, "No Jesus, no peace; Know Jesus, know peace." It may seem simplistic, but it is so true. Jesus Christ is the only way that this world and its inhabitants will ever know peace. Until He comes again and balances the scales of injustice, the only ones without war will be those who have His peace in their hearts. We can pray for an end to war, for no true Christian would want such carnage. But when we pray such a prayer we are praying for Christ to come. His is the only true solution to the battles that plague our world.

Being Christ to Our World

When the Lamb opened the third seal, I heard the third living creature say, "Come!" I looked, and there before me was a black horse! Its rider was holding a pair of scales in his hand. Then I heard what sounded like a voice among the four living creatures, saying, "A quart of wheat for a day's wages, and three quarts of barley for a day's wages, and do not damage the oil and the wine!" (6:5-6)

The opening of the third seal brings about a black horse. Its rider carries a weighing scales and he weighs grain, representing the famine that would accompany the war brought about by the opening of the previous seals. Grain would scarcely be available, and wheat would be three times as expensive as barley. There seems to be no scarcity of oil and wine. They would be abundant, although bread would be in short supply. It would seem that some men would always rather have liquor than food. The main emphasis of this part of the vision is that the necessities of the poor will be in short supply, but the luxuries of the rich will not cease. Jesus told us that we would always have the poor with us (Matthew 26:11) and it would seem that the rich will continue to profit from them.

The question is as old as the book of Job. Why do the wicked prosper and the righteous suffer? It's not an easy question to answer, except that we have to understand that when God created man with a free will, He left the consequences of man's choices in man's hands. When people choose to satisfy his or her own desires selfishly there are always those who will suffer deprivation and lack as a result.

The Christian response is to counter selfishness with love. Love will win in the end. Suffering around us can be the greatest opportunity to really act as the body of Christ. When pain comes, let's not miss our chance to represent Him.

Death is an Opportunity

When the Lamb opened the fourth seal, I heard the voice of the fourth living creature say, "Come!" I looked, and there before me was a pale horse! Its rider was named Death, and Hades was following close behind him. They were given power over a fourth of the earth to kill by sword, famine and plague, and by the wild beasts of the earth. (6:7-8)

We see the fourth seal opening and a pale horse appearing. Death is its rider and the grave (Hades) was right behind him. The end of this seal is the natural result of the other three. War produces casualties, and the Church is not exempt from the pains of battle. Again we must note that this rider was "given" his power. Even death is subject to the victor over death—Jesus Christ.

So many people look at these horses and riders as something that lies out there in the future—at the end of the age. They are often referred to as "The Four Horsemen of the Apocalypse," but they are not someday. They are now! John is describing what has been going on and will be going on until the second coming of Jesus. Invasions, war, famine, and death are a part of our world that has chosen self-rule instead of God's rule.

We have a choice. We can throw up our hands in despair at the state of the world or we can roll up our sleeves and do something about it. We may not reach everyone, but we can reach one. Not everyone will listen to the words of the gospel, but some will. Where sin abounds grace can abound much more. The darkest days are the brightest opportunities to bring others into the light of Christ. War, famine, pestilence, and death are a part of what we experience on this place we call earth. It is the natural result of sin and what the enemy has been plotting since his beginning. It is also when the Church has its finest hour for ministry in Jesus name.

Let God Handle It

When he opened the fifth seal, I saw under the altar the souls of those who had been slain because of the word of God and the testimony they had maintained. They called out in a loud voice, "How long, Sovereign Lord, holy and true, until you judge the inhabitants of the earth and avenge our blood?" Then each of them was given a white robe, and they were told to wait a little longer, until the number of their fellow servants and brothers who were to be killed as they had been was completed. (6:9-11)

This fifth seal reveals the results of the war and devastation described in the opening of the first four seals. The persecutions that made martyrs of those seen beneath the altar were most likely the work of Nero and his successors. These souls cry out for justice but must wait until more saints also follow in their path. Each one is given a white robe of purity and a reward of rest until the end of time. The end is determined by the will of God, but the death of His saints will not be in vain. Those of all ages who have died for the faith are represented here, and we can take heart that God is faithful and will not forsake them.

Sometimes we are tempted to take matters into our own hands and take revenge on those who hurt us. This is a natural reaction, but it is not a Christian one. The way of Christ is to follow the example of Christ, even to the point of turning the other cheek and praying for our enemies. By doing so, we show the world we are true children of God.

This is often easier said than done, however. Even if we can endure being abused by someone, it gets much harder to wait for God's justice when the abuse involves someone in our family or someone who is very close to us. It is at this point that we must remember that God is in charge and He has a plan. Our suffering and theirs will not last forever. There is coming a day of reckoning when God will say, "Enough!" For now, we must be people of faith, not people of sight.

No One is His Equal

I watched as he opened the sixth seal. There was a great earthquake. The sun turned black like sackcloth made of goat hair, the whole moon turned blood red, and the stars in the sky fell to earth, as late figs drop from a fig tree when shaken by a strong wind. The sky receded like a scroll, rolling up, and every mountain and island was removed from its place. Then the kings of the earth, the princes, the generals, the rich, the mighty, and every slave and every free man hid in caves and among the rocks of the mountains. They called to the mountains and the rocks, "Fall on us and hide us from the face of him who sits on the throne and from the wrath of the Lamb! For the great day of their wrath has come, and who can stand?" (6:12-17)

In the first four seals, one of the four living creatures calls for the coming of the described events. In the opening of the last three seals, no creature is mentioned. Each creature is merely beckoning the four horsemen to come. In the opening of this seal, the destruction of war is followed by an earthquake. Up to this time, human instruments as the agents of God have brought about the devastations. Now nature itself is used for judgment upon mankind.

The description of the universe in upheaval is a repetition of the words of Jesus in Matthew 24:29-30; Luke 21:20-36; and Mark 13:24-26. The prophet Joel had echoed these thoughts in Joel 2:31. The Church was familiar with this kind of teaching. The ravages of nature are not coincidence. They are part of the judgment of God on a disobedient world. Nature is a warning siren, trying to get mankind's attention turned back to the Almighty.

At the time of the end, kings, military men, strong men, and common men will shake with fright, because it will become apparent that they are confronting the wrath of God. It has been said that there are no atheists in foxholes. There are also no brave, independent men in the presence of God. His justice is always perfect. Now is the time to live for Him before it will be too late.

Even the Winds Obey

After this I saw four angels standing at the four corners of the earth, holding back the four winds of the earth to prevent any wind from blowing on the land or on the sea or on any tree. (7:1)

This chapter serves as an interlude between the sixth and seventh seals, but also as a reminder for the Church as to what lies in store for them. The fate of the redeemed stands in stark contrast to the universal upheaval that is described in the closing verses of chapter six. In this part of the vision, we see the sealing of the saints on earth as well as the picture of all the ransomed people of all ages as they stand before the throne and the Lamb. This chapter answers the question, "What is the fate of the believers as a result of the terrible happenings just described in chapter six?"

Four angels appear at the four corners of the earth. This is not to imply that the world is actually flat (though this was the common thought in John's time), but refers to the directions of a map (i.e., north, south, east, west). The four winds are the counterparts of the four horsemen and are seen throughout the Old Testament and the Apocrypha as agents of destruction. Zechariah's four horsemen are specifically interpreted as "the four winds of the heavens." (For further references see Zechariah 6:5; Psalm 69:33; Isaiah 19:1; 66:15.) Winds are a natural symbol of destruction (Jeremiah 4:11ff; 49:36; 51:1ff).

The angels of the winds could cause destruction on "the earth, on the sea, or upon any tree." These angels are seen to be holding back the winds from being destructive. John, being a good Jew as well as a good Christian, ascribes all activity as under the control of the Father. Even the winds cannot blow without His command. We should take comfort in such mighty power.

God's Seal of Approval

Then I saw another angel coming up from the east, having the seal of the living God. He called out in a loud voice to the four angels who had been given power to harm the land and the sea: "Do not harm the land or the sea or the trees until we put a seal on the foreheads of the servants of our God." (7:2-3)

A fifth angel appears with a command for the other four. He is said to be coming out of the east. The direction is symbolic, for out of the east comes light. Out of the east came the wise men with the news that the Christ had been born. Paradise was set in the east (Genesis 2:8); the glory of God comes to the temple from the east (Ezekiel 43:2); and the return of the Messiah is expected from the east (Matthew 24:27). The east is seen as the source of God's light and blessing.

This angel carries the seal of the living God. The seal was basically a mark of ownership. This was very important in an age when most men could not read. The symbolism goes back to Ezekiel's vision of 9:1ff, where a man with an inkhorn is told to go throughout Jerusalem and put a mark on the foreheads of the righteous so that they would be spared from the agents of destruction.

The angel gives the command for the four angels of the destructive winds to hold back until the servants of God have God's seal on their foreheads so that they will not be victims of the violent force. The seal of God is for those who have utter devotion for the cause of Christ. The seal is a sign that these people belong to God and are under His power and authority. This is not something that comes at the end of the age. It is a reality that we experience when we come to Christ in faith. It will not wash off and cannot be diluted. If you are a Christian, you have the seal of God on your life. Praise the Lord!

We've Got a Big Family

Then I heard the number of those who were sealed: 144,000 from all the tribes of Israel. From the tribe of Judah 12,000 were sealed, from the tribe of Reuben 12,000, from the tribe of Gad 12,000, from the tribe of Asher 12,000, from the tribe of Naphtali 12,000, from the tribe of Manasseh 12,000, from the tribe of Simeon 12,000, from the tribe of Levi 12,000, from the tribe of Issachar 12,000, from the tribe of Zebulun 12,000, from the tribe of Joseph 12,000, from the tribe of Benjamin 12,000. (7:4-8)

John hears the number of those who were sealed. There are various interpretations as to the meaning of the 144,000, but in keeping with the context of the whole New Testament account, it is rational to assume that the number is not a literal figure, but is a symbol of the Christian Church, or as the Apostle Paul would say, "the true Jew" (Romans 2:29), and "the Israel of God" (Galatians 6:16). Any attempts to make this number apply to some certain select group of Christians or Jews must be rejected. The number 144,000 stands, not for limitation but for completion and perfection. It is made up of twelve multiplied by twelve times 1000—the perfect square. This does not tell us that the number of the saved will be very small; it tells us that the number of the saved will be very large. What a message of encouragement for the Church of John's day—and ours!

We sometimes think that when Jesus said in Matthew 7:14, "But small is the gate and narrow the road that leads to life, and only a few find it," he meant that heaven's inhabitants would be few in number. However, the Lord is still adding to His Church daily, and when we are united with the saints of all ages it's going to be a crowd with a number to stagger the imagination.

The Church is still growing. People of all colors, languages, and backgrounds are our brothers and sisters. What a joy it will be to spend eternity with them.

One in Christ

After this I looked and there before me was a great multitude that no one could count, from every nation, tribe, people and language, standing before the throne and in front of the Lamb. They were wearing white robes and were holding palm branches in their hands. (7:9)

To help make the previous point complete, John proceeds to paint an unforgettable picture of a vast crowd of people from every nation on earth that are now in the bliss of heaven. They are free from pain, anxiety, and sorrow. The only difference between this group and the 144,000 is the fact that the 144,000 were still on earth. The group of this verse are the redeemed of heaven. They are too many to number and come from every culture and section of the world. They wear white robes of purity and wave their palms of victory.

In our world today we hear continually of tribal conflicts, political posturing, and ethnic segregation. On the other side, however, there will be none of that. We who are in Christ can look forward to a world that is made up of people from all parts of the globe and from all ages of time. There will not be groups of Americans, Africans, Asians, or Europeans. There will be no Nazarenes, Baptists, Methodists, Protestants or Catholics. In Christ we will all one, and that union and unity will be perfect there.

Don't let anyone deceive you and tell you that a certain group is the only group of true believers or that one ethnic group is better than another. All are equal at the foot of the cross of Christ, and all eternity will be lived out as the brotherhood of man. One of the great joys of being a part of a world ministry is to see this scene in an embryonic stage. Christ prayed that we would be one and as time goes on that prayer is being answered.

Get Ready to Praise

And they cried out in a loud voice: "Salvation belongs to our God, who sits on the throne, and to the Lamb. All the angels were standing around the throne and around the elders and the four living creatures. They fell down on their faces before the throne and worshiped God, saying: "Amen! Praise and glory and wisdom and thanks and honor and power and strength be to our God for ever and ever. Amen!" (7:10-12)

The heavenly redeemed sing out in praise to God and to the Lamb! Salvation has come to them through the sovereign act of God in Christ. Once again a great praise session breaks out. The participants are not only the saints who have been redeemed, but include also the angels, the elders, and the living creatures that surround the throne. They give an echo to the first chorus of praise as the attributes of God (glory, wisdom, honor, power, and strength) are extolled.

There was an old saint whom I once pastored who continually reminded me that we were always behind in our praise. How right he was. We could shout from the housetops our adoration for all God has done for the rest of our lives and never be able to muster the praise that He deserves. Sadly, however, many are content to show up for church and watch the music leaders perform and never learn what it is like to give praise to God from their own hearts.

There are many disagreements about what the life to come will be like, but there is one thing upon which all Christians agree. To be in the presence of the Almighty is to be in a place that is filled with praise. I like to think of this as the "Eternal Praise Party!" The "Praise Party" never stops, and if we plan to be there someday we may as well get used to getting in on it here. We truly are behind in our praise, so let's start making up for it beginning with today!

The Great Tribulation

Then one of the elders asked me, "These in white robes—who are they, and where did they come from?" I answered, "Sir, you know." And he said, "These are they who have come out of the great tribulation; they have washed their robes and made them white in the blood of the Lamb. (7:13-14)

John is asked by one of the twenty-four elders if he understands who these people are and where they have come from. John throws the question back to the elder and then the elder begins his explanation. He tells John that these people are those who have come out of the great time of tribulation. This refers to the constant tribulation of life, which was the result of evil's battle against the Church. These Christians have come through the battles victoriously, because they have purified themselves (*washed their robes*) through the cleansing blood of the Lamb. On their own they could never have survived—nor can we—but through the magnificent power of Christ we can be overcomers in the face of every trial and tribulation.

If we are looking for specific years of tribulation to arrive at the end of the age then we miss completely what John is saying. Many in the Western world have never had any kind of hardship put upon them for their faith, because they live in a country where freedom of worship is usually, sadly, taken for granted. However, much of the world has lived for centuries in great oppression because of faith in Jesus Christ as the Savior of the world. Try telling those who have been jailed, tortured, raped, mutilated, and killed for their Christian faith that they have not been through great tribulation. This tribulation refers to what Christians face in life here on earth. All who stand for Christ will be tested and all who overcome will be rewarded with life eternal.

Home at Last

Therefore, "they are before the throne of God and serve him day and night in his temple; and he who sits on the throne will spread his tent over them. Never again will they hunger; never again will they thirst. The sun will not beat upon them, nor any scorching heat. For the Lamb at the center of the throne will be their shepherd; he will lead them to springs of living water. And God will wipe away every tear from their eyes." (7:15-17)

As a result of the cleansing blood of Christ, the redeemed of God have been granted the honor of abiding in the presence of God eternally. They have direct access to Him and serve Him continually in His perfect kingdom (*temple*). Heaven is not a place of idle laziness, but a cathedral of service and praise. God will spread His glory over His people like a tent, and never again will those who have crossed over to the heavenly realms have to deal with hunger, thirst, or pain. They will be free from all torment. The Lamb, who abides on the throne, will give them the living water of which songs and psalms have been written. All grief will be swallowed up in the new creation, and there will no longer be any reason for sorrow.

The eternal bliss of the righteous is set in contrast to the plagues, tribulations, and martyrdom they endured while here on earth. They are contrasted to the fate of the great men of earth who are heard to beg for death in preference to facing the wrath of God. John is making no attempt here to use scare tactics to evangelize the earth, but uses the comparisons to encourage and strengthen the Church of Jesus Christ. No one is scared into a loving relationship, and to use the scriptures of this book in such a way does immeasurable harm to the context in which they were written. Love is always a draw and fear is always divisive. No wonder we are drawn to a God who is pure love.

Preaching Outside the Box

When he opened the seventh seal, there was silence in heaven for about half an hour. And I saw the seven angels who stand before God, and to them were given seven trumpets. (8:1-2)

In the midst of the joyous celebration in heaven, John takes us back to the seals. The final seal is opened. We have seen the end of both the righteous and the wicked; so one would possibly wonder what more there is to say. The seventh seal brings us into the third vision and into another unfolding drama. While we may expect to have come to the end of history and the final victory, instead we find ourselves looking down still upon a wicked and rebellious world. The visions of the trumpets, like that of the seals, carry us back to the beginning and once more we move across the troubled course of history.

As chapter eight begins with the opening of the seventh seal, it is followed by a dramatic pause in heaven for what seems to be thirty minutes. The sheer stillness is even more effective than the thunder and lightning. From the context of what follows, the stilling of voices is needed in order that the prayers of the saints may be heard.

Seven trumpets are given to seven angels that stand before God. In the writings of the Old and New Testaments, the trumpet is always the symbol of the intervention of God in history (Exodus 19:16, 19; Isaiah 27:13; Joel 2:1; Zephaniah 1:16; Zechariah 9:9-14; I Corinthians 15:52-53; I Thessalonians 4:16).

God always helps his servants find new ways to tell the old story. Here John sets an example for us to think outside of the box to present the gospel message. Our job is not to change the story, but to present it in such a way as to get attention of a new generation. That's what John is doing in his day.

The Impact of Prayer

Another angel, who had a golden censer, came and stood at the altar. He was given much incense to offer, with the prayers of all the saints, on the golden altar before the throne. The smoke of the incense, together with the prayers of the saints, went up before God from the angel's hand. (8:3-4)

Another angel appears and before the first seven can blow their horns, the prayers of the saints are offered. This is an important verse. John means us to see that the prayers of God's people are supremely important. Incense is offered with the prayers, which we may take to symbolize the unity of the worship of heaven and earth. The golden censer and the golden altar show us the value of the prayers. The time for answering of the prayers of the saints for God's judgment upon sin has come. God will vindicate the cause of the righteous.

As the smoke and prayers rise up to God we are reminded that prayer is not the lonely task it so often feels. There is heavenly assistance and our prayers do reach God.

I heard a great preacher once say that a good sermon on prayer will put anyone under conviction. The more we pray the more we need to pray. The more we pray the more our hearts hunger to be united with the one to whom we are praying.

It's good to know that our prayers are not just empty words that go nowhere. Here we see that they are incense before God and they rise directly to His throne. God is aware of each prayer that is breathed and cares about what we care about. So, pray on—and pray boldly and confidently! The Lord of all is interested in hearing what we have to say and is able to do exceedingly abundantly more than we can imagine in response.

Prayer and Judgment

Then the angel took the censer, filled it with fire from the altar, and hurled it on the earth; and there came peals of thunder, rumblings, flashes of lightning and an earthquake. (8:5)

Fire comes from the very altar on which the prayers of the saints have been offered. This surely means that the prayers of God's people play a necessary part in ushering in the judgments of God. As fire from the altar descends upon the earth, the silence is now broken. There are thunders and voices, lightning, and an earthquake, which are the symbolic warnings of the judgments about to come. The trumpets are warnings of judgment and calls to repentance and they are an answer to the prayers of God's people.

Have you ever considered how much your prayers have to do with the judgments of God? Could it be that God is just waiting for His people to ask before He does anything? It's an amazing concept, but I think that we will find when we reach the other side that we have had much more authority than we have taken advantage of and that we truly do not have because we have not asked of the Father.

As the angels prepare to blow their trumpets we notice that as with the seals, there is a distinction between the first four and the last three. Here the four are largely concerned with the forces of nature and the last three trumpets are directed at men. If prayers are the driving force behind what happens next, then we too have a direct role in how the judgments of God are being played out on our world. This is not a "someday" text. This is a call for the people of God to pray and pray now!

The Third Vision: Revelation 8:6-11:19

After the opening of the final seal we move back across history to the Church age. The opening of the seventh seal produces the coming of seven angels with seven trumpets. Before the trumpets are blown the prayers of the saints are noted, showing the importance of prayer to God.

1. **The first trumpet** – Brings blight on a part of the land. God uses things like dust storms to bring judgment on the land. (8:7)
2. **The second trumpet** – Brings disaster on a part of the sea. God uses maritime catastrophes to call for repentance. (8:8-9)
3. **The third trumpet** – Brings a crisis on a part of the fresh water supply. God uses water emergencies to remind people of the need to repent. (8:10-11)
4. **The fourth trumpet** – Brings a plague on the daylight. God uses eclipses of the heavenly bodies to call men to Himself. (8:12-13)

- The troubles in nature are about to intensify. The first four trumpets had to do with the judgment of God on the physical world. The next three will be spiritual in nature.

5. **The fifth trumpet** – The fallen star is a symbol of Satan. The terrors coming on the earth are beyond nature; they are demonic. The pit of the abyss is being opened and supernatural terrors are being poured out upon the world. (9:1-12)

- The fifth trumpet says that God's people have been sealed and great mental confusion and spiritual disillusionment will come on a godless world. One has only to look around to see how this trumpet is even today sounding all around the world.

6. **The sixth trumpet** – This trumpet is to be interpreted along the lines of the preceding trumpet, but now everything is

greatly intensified. Instead of torment there is death, and instead of locusts there is a huge army of fiery horsemen on strange steeds. (9:13–11:14)
- One would expect the world to see what horrible things sin is doing and turn their hearts to the Lord, but the result is just the opposite. Hard times don't always drive people to their knees. Usually hard times just make people harder against God. They continue their demonic practice of worshipping their man-made gods. Men go deeper in sin when they refuse to yield to the call of God on their lives. Men without God hold on to the things of the world at all costs.
- At the end of chapter nine there is an interlude that asks what is happening to the Church during the blowing of the trumpets of God's wrath and judgment. Chapters ten and eleven give us the answer. 10:1–11:14 comes between the sixth and seventh trumpet just as chapter seven is placed between the sixth and seventh seals. These are times of assuring the Church of her safety in the midst of all the judgments of God on a sinful world.
7. **The seventh trumpet** – Judgment is complete and we return to the great praise party that is going on in the presence of God. (11:15–19)

Praying Up a Storm

Then the seven angels who had the seven trumpets prepared to sound them. The first angel sounded his trumpet, and there came hail and fire mixed with blood, and it was hurled down upon the earth. A third of the earth was burned up, a third of the trees were burned up, and all the green grass was burned up. (8:6-7)

The sounding of the first trumpet brings blight upon the land. The destruction is only partial however, and that partial destruction is a solemn warning. Every judgment of God is a call to repentance. John sees the catastrophes of nature not as a meteorologist, but as a prophet. The blood mixed with hail and fire could possibly present the picture of a terrific electrical storm and God is riding upon the storm.

Have you ever prayed for God to use nature to open the eyes of those who are blind to His place in this world? Children are often afraid of storms because all they see is the lightning and hear the thunder and the howling of the winds. Certainly these events can be very fierce at times. But if we assure our young that the forces of nature are wake-up calls for a wayward world, it will not only direct them to the importance of entering into a relationship with the Almighty, but also comfort them as they realize that He sends the storms to urge others to acknowledge His greatness. Every storm is an opportunity to see His glory, whether it is of the literal physical variety or just one of the many storms of life we face. They are indicator marks. They point to the Master and to His endless and almighty power. As we cannot stop a storm we also can never stop His judgments upon those who continue to refuse to acknowledge Him.

God is in Control

The second angel sounded his trumpet, and something like a huge mountain, all ablaze, was thrown into the sea. A third of the sea turned into blood, a third of the living creatures in the sea died, and a third of the ships were destroyed. (8:8-9)

The second trumpet affects the sea. Interpreters have sometimes attempted to work out all the details of such symbolism and have often reached some grotesque conclusions. The judgment upon nature could very easily be a volcanic eruption into the sea. We should remember that symbols are not pictures. They are suggestions that appeal to the imagination. John is not referring to particular person and events. He is simply giving up a symbolic and dramatic portrayal of the whole course of human history. The significance of this destruction is that it has come from God.

It has been noted that three-fourths of the planet we live on is covered by water. Would it not seem reasonable that the Lord of the land is not also Lord of the sea? Whenever something happens or has happened upon the waves it is again a picture of the hand of God calling people unto Himself. His judgments are not out of His anger against mankind, but are demonstrations of His power and remember—they are in answer to the prayers of His saints.

Certainly there is a feeling of the mysterious about all of this. His ways are beyond our ways and beyond our understanding, yet we can take comfort in His great mercy and grace toward us. With a whisper of His will He can remove mountains and churn the waters of the deep, yet He cares about us. He cares enough to flex His muscle occasionally to remind us as to whom is still in control of this old world of ours.

Judgments for the Good of Man

The third angel sounded his trumpet, and a great star, blazing like a torch, fell from the sky on a third of the rivers and on the springs of water—the name of the star is Wormwood. A third of the waters turned bitter, and many people died from the waters that had become bitter. (8:10-11)

As the previous trumpet affected salt water, this trumpet troubles the fresh water of the earth. Here, in symbolism, the judgment is intensified. The scene is of a meteor, but its impact is to be understood theologically. It is reminiscent of the Egyptian plagues, where men could not drink the water. Twice in the prophecies of Jeremiah the Word of the Lord is recorded, "I will feed this people wormwood and give them poisonous water to drink" (9:15; 23:15). The main thrust of the passage is concerned with the effects of the water upon men. John's main concern is the punishment of the ungodly.

Just as there have been storms at sea that were fierce and caused men to climb out in terror, so also the world has at many times recorded crises concerning it's fresh water supply. Many lands are suffering droughts from lack of fresh water and climatologists have predicted that wars of the future may not be nearly so much over oil as over water. We know it is needed for life and when it is scarce men begin to fight over what little there is of it.

John is trying to point people to the fact that even problems with obtaining fresh water are messages from the throne of God. These are judgments that come upon men in answer to the prayers of men. God uses these judgments as calls for mankind to turn back to Him. Like parents who care about their children, God administers justice to open the eyes of the inhabitants of this world. He cares about us that much!

Example from the Darkness

The fourth angel sounded his trumpet, and a third of the sun was struck, a third of the moon, and a third of the stars, so that a third of them turned dark. A third of the day was without light, and also a third of the night. (8:12)

The fourth trumpet brings blight upon the light causing a plague of darkness. Here again, the Egyptian plague comes to mind. Times of literal and physical darkness have often settled upon the world. John wishes to affirm that men experience the darkness in the day and intensified darkness in the night as a result of their sins. There have been times when the sun was eclipsed, when Christ was concealed, when the Church was under a shadow, when the Bible was obscured, and deep darkness covered the face of the earth. But Christ lives on and His Church continues. Until He returns there will be darkness, but it will never put out His divine light. The message of the first four trumpets is clear. God uses nature to send messages to men.

The world has often accused "religion" and sometimes "the Church" for all the ills that often plague society. There is no doubt that to a certain extent that this is true. However, it is not the true Church that is the cause of pain, but the false imitation of it. It comes from the darkness that is reflected in religious fervor without love and causes without compassion. True Christianity has always been about light because it is about God and God is light (I John 1:5).

We must remember that John is writing in symbols, not about literal occurrences. The darkness is real, but it is darkness that covers minds and corrupts souls. As we walk in the light of God there is no fear of these judgments for the child of God.

Pacing the Story

As I watched, I heard an eagle that was flying in midair call out in a loud voice: "Woe! Woe! Woe to the inhabitants of the earth, because of the trumpet blasts about to be sounded by the other three angels!" (8:13)

This verse marks an interlude in the sequence of the trumpets. John sees and hears a flying eagle that is calling out a warning about the coming trumpets. The solemn words of the eagle show that the plagues to come are worse than those the world has already experienced. There is a deepening of intensity.

The last three woes are spiritual rather than material. The seventh trumpet blast is delayed, as was the opening of the seventh seal. It appears three chapters later in 11:15. As we read this book carefully we will see how it is not told in a linear fashion, but in a spiral of seven visions. It is not to be read like a newspaper, but more like poetry played out in a mini-series.

John, inspired by the Holy Spirit, uses different paces to tell his stories. The message is the same throughout the book, but through repetition, imagery, and the painting of word pictures he pulls the reader along from event to event in wonder.

We should be thankful for how God uses the gifts and talents of those He inspires. Just as some build great buildings and bridges, while others delve into microscopic mysteries, God also inspires writers to write words that will last forever. Here is John's way of saying, "Wake up! God is about to say something of which you need to take note!" The opening of the seals and the blowing of the trumpets tell the same story, but now it is going to go into more detail. John may be an ordinary man, but he is transformed into a master communicator by the power of the Spirit—the same power that can transform us still.

Evil is Alive in Our World

The fifth angel sounded his trumpet, and I saw a star that had fallen from the sky to the earth. The star was given the key to the shaft of the Abyss. (9:1)

The first of the last three woes surpasses the judgments of the earlier trumpets. It is more severe and is different in character. With the blowing of the fifth trumpet we begin the third vision and have the entrance of Satanic and demonic forces. This passage is described in great symbolism and greatly helps with our understanding of God. He not only communicates His message to men (1:1), rules over His creation (4:1ff), is in control over history (5:1ff) and the forces of nature (8:7-12), but He is also in authority over demonic forces (chapter 9). God uses these forces in this chapter to bring plagues of a mental and spiritual nature upon godless men.

The fallen star is a symbol of Satan. The terrors coming upon the earth are beyond nature; they are demonic. The pit of the abyss is being opened and supernatural terrors are being poured out upon the world. The evil spirit, or Satan, opens up the abyss, which most likely stands for the *sheol* of the Old Testament (the place of the dead). This whole passage follows the image of Joel 1-2 to a great extent.

It must be noted here that the fallen star was "given" a key to the abyss. The One on the throne has delegated whatever authority the evil one possesses to him. Satan is not an equal adversary with God. He is only one of the Father's lowly minions.

Today we can know that victory over even demons is ours through the blood of our Lord and Savior, Jesus Christ. All things are under His authority.

Protected By the Seal

When he opened the Abyss, smoke rose from it like the smoke from a gigantic furnace. The sun and sky were darkened by the smoke from the Abyss. And out of the smoke locusts came down upon the earth and were given power like that of scorpions of the earth. They were told not to harm the grass of the earth or any plant or tree, but only those people who did not have the seal of God on their foreheads. (9:2-4)

As the pit is opened a terrific smoke pours out of it until it encompasses all light. There is no part of the earth that has not been touched by the effects of the evil one.

Out of the smoke come grotesque and appalling creatures that have the appearance of locusts. These locusts have the power to cause pain however. John most likely relates these locust-like images to scorpions because in actuality they are demons that thrive on bringing pain to men.

Thankfully, the power of these creatures is limited. They are only to torment those who do not have the seal of God on their foreheads (7:4). The fallen star that has the key to the bottomless pit is in contrast to "the bright and morning star" (2:28; 22:16), who has "the key of David" (3:7) and complete authority over death and the grave. The 144,000 of 7:4 are the whole Church. All the saints of God are safe from the demonic powers. They have been marked with the seal of divine ownership and protection. Since the demons were told that they could not "harm the grass of the earth or any plant of tree" we are essentially told that this present judgment is different from the woes of the previous trumpets. This judgment is not material, or physical, but spiritual.

Demons can plague the minds of unbelievers continually, but the people of God can rest in the grace that conquers even the powers of darkness.

Affliction of the Mind

They were not given power to kill them, but only to torture them for five months. And the agony they suffered was like that of the sting of a scorpion when it strikes a man. (9:5)

The plague is to last for five months. John could have been relating this to the five months of summer, since that is when locusts are expected to appear. The life span of a locust from birth, through the larva stage to death, is five months. More than likely, however, the five months stand for a brief, indefinite period—as God measures time. The locusts are not to have the power to kill, but to cause intense suffering. This in itself tells us that the affliction is not physical, but mental and spiritual. The agony is as severe as a scorpion sting, but cannot lead to the same result. John is making apparent to us what we should call the "ethical" significance of the coming troubles—the spiritual values that are being determined by the last three plagues. He is no longer concerned with the judgment of the destructive action against nature. That was the theme of 8:6–12. Now he is dealing with the mental and spiritual anguish that sin brings.

One thing that is apparent as we push on into the twenty-first century is the growing need for counselors to combat the skyrocketing cases of mental illness. Though it is not fair to say that all mental illness is caused by demons, it is fair to say that many that are plagued in the mind are so afflicted because of their openness to sin. Sin is the destroyer and Christ is the Redeemer. The choice seems simple.

John's call to believers is for them to be aware of the enemy's schemes. We are here to be salt and light, combating the wiles of the wicked one. He is not an illusion, but neither is Christ's power in us to be victorious.

A Life or Death Matter

During those days men will seek death, but will not find it; they will long to die, but death will elude them. (9:6)

Because of the torment of these creatures "men will seek death," but death will not come to them. John most likely had in mind the torturing of the human conscience. Job speaks of the supreme misery of those who long for death and it won't come (Job 3:21). Jeremiah speaks of the day when men will choose death rather than life (Jeremiah 8:3). On more occasions than I care to count I have had people sitting in my office for counseling or talking to me on the phone who has said the words, "I just wish I could die." Most were not really considering suicide, but their life was such as horrible wreck that they welcomed death as a solution to the mess sin had made in it.

This is why Christ came. He came to bring hope to the hopeless and care to the careless. He wants us to cast our cares on Him so that He can begin to mend the broken pieces of our lives. He promised us life more abundant (John 10:10) and that means more than just enduring the circumstances in which we find ourselves.

Certainly there are some people who seem to have been given an unfair shake in life, but this passage is specifically talking about those who have been closed to the things of God and opened to the things of the world. Demons plague the mind that is without Christ. All the pills, drugs, sex, and pursuit of personal gratification will never replace the peace that can only come from Jesus. As an old song says, "He is still the answer for your soul." Men who don't seek life seek death, whether they realize they are doing it or not.

Immunity from Scorpions

The locusts looked like horses prepared for battle. On their heads they wore something like crowns of gold, and their faces resembled human faces. Their hair was like women's hair, and their teeth were like lions' teeth. They had breastplates like breastplates of iron, and the sound of their wings was like the thundering of many horses and chariots rushing into battle. They had tails and stings like scorpions, and in their tails they had power to torment people for five months. (9:7-10)

The locusts are given a strange description. Many writers have tried to find an explanation for every detail of the symbolism—even to the tails, the hair, and the faces of these demons. More often than not all they succeed in doing is to cloud the context and confuse the reader. It is better to take this passage as a depiction of demonic influence in history, whose agents are thick as locusts, fearful as lions, intelligent as men, wily as women, malicious as scorpions, whose purpose is to cause a state of spiritual and mental disorder and make life a living death. These creatures are not to be identified with any particular person or period in time. The trumpets of judgment were blowing in John's day and they are still blowing in our day also.

We do not want to underestimate the power of these enemies of our souls, nor do we want to fear them. We who are in Christ are made secure by His blood and no child of God ever will be let down by Him. As John said it so well, "the one who is in you is greater than the one that is in the world" (I John 4:4). Since that is the case, we who are in Christ depend on His power to protect us from the plots and attacks from the enemy of our souls. The secular inhabitants of this world will feel the pain of his attacks and certainly even that will cause grief to those of us who care about others. However, in Christ we are secure and the "scorpions" of life cannot harm us.

Satan is on the March, but Christ is on the Throne

They had as king over them the angel of the Abyss, whose name in Hebrew is Abaddon, and in Greek, Apollyon. (9:11)

"Abaddon" is Hebrew for "destruction" and "Apollyon" is the present participle of the Greek verb "to destroy" and means "the destroyer." It is fitting that the king of the demons should be called by both the names "Destruction" and "The Destroyer." John's readers would see the symbolism of the impending destruction that awaits the ungodly.

The fifth trumpet says that after God's people have been sealed, great mental confusion and spiritual disillusionment will come on a godless world. One has only to look around to see this trumpet is even today sounding all around the world.

In every generation evil is on the march. Though Satan was defeated convincingly by Christ at Calvary, forever protecting those who trust in His name, his influence is still felt by masses of people who have not been "sealed" by the Redeemer. As we watch the news reports and see killings, drug abuse, families in disarray, and society in turmoil we see evil personified. How sad to see so many people who are still susceptible to Satan's wiles that could be free if only they would seek divine grace.

The enemy of our soul is a destroyer. He never tires of trying to ruin our lives. The angel of the Abyss is a bloodthirsty murderer. All who trust in themselves or in the things of this world for their security are open to his schemes. The converse is that those who confess their sins and turn to Christ will join the sanctuary of the "sealed in Christ."

Protection from the Woes

The first woe is past; two other woes are yet to come. The sixth angel sounded his trumpet, and I heard a voice coming from the horns of the golden altar that is before God. (9:12-13)

In 8:13 the eagle proclaimed that three woes were coming. This verse is a separation between the first and the second woe, to be followed by a third.

As the sixth trumpet is blown, John hears a voice coming from the horns (which stands for strength) of the golden altar. In 6:10 the martyrs cried to God from under the altar and in 8:3-5 prayers were offered on it. Judgment was released as a result. It is likely that the prayers of God's people are still on John's mind. Prayer brought on the first judgments and also brings forth these judgments. John doesn't want his readers to forget that prayer is a mighty force.

Who can imagine what power the prayers of God's people unleash? Repeatedly Jesus taught His disciples to emphasize the importance of prayer. Continually we see in Jesus Himself the value of a life wrapped up in God. John is making the same statement through his writing here. The judgments of God come about as a result of the prayers of God's people. Just as we can pray down a safety hedge around those who follow after Christ we can also pray for God to rightly judge those who would do them wrongly.

Knowing this information, it is baffling why so many Christians spend so little time and emphasis in their own lives on prayer. If prayer can move mountains, change lives, and bring about justice, perhaps it is time that we lay down our pickets signs and end our protest marches, and instead organize the Church to pray—for that is where real power lies.

The Price of Removing God's Restraint

It said to the sixth angel who had the trumpet, "Release the four angels who are bound at the great river Euphrates." And the four angels who had been kept ready for this very hour and day and month and year were released to kill a third of mankind. (9:14-15)

The voice calls of the sixth angel with the trumpet to release the four other angels. The fact that they have been bound appears to show that they are not good angels going forth voluntarily to do God's will. They are evil beings that have been held in check until now. This fits the general pattern that this section of the book deals with the demonic.

The loosing of the four angels that were bound at the Euphrates River follows the sixth trumpet. The Euphrates River was the boundary, Israel's line of defense against her enemies. In the eighth chapter of Isaiah it is the symbol of the Assyrians. The loosing of the angels signifies that God's permission is given for the avenging hoards to rush in. God's restraint is removed and destruction overflows the land. The whole picture symbolizes the upheavals and terrors that prefaces the coming of Christ and brings us down again to the end of the Christian era. Just as locust tortured men in the previous trumpet, now the angels are deadly. It is a warning for the world to repent, but John sadly reports that men do not do it.

It is at God's appointed time, according to God's divine plan, that the angels of destruction are released. If John intends to impress and terrify, he is successful in his efforts. Divine judgment is no laughing matter and we see that a large number of mankind—though not the majority—are to fall as a result of God's wrath. God is on the throne and the final word will be His.

Judgment of Pain

The number of the mounted troops was two hundred million. I heard their number. The horses and riders I saw in my vision looked like this: Their breastplates were fiery red, dark blue, and yellow as sulfur. The heads of the horses resembled the heads of lions, and out of their mouths came fire, smoke and sulfur. (9:16-17)

An army follows the angels and the size of the demonic host is inconceivable. John could not count them, so he had to be told their number. It is difficult to believe that a literal number is intended; the demonic hosts are simply like the grains of sand on the seashore.

John gives us a new description of the demonic horses and their riders. He reminds us that these are not natural horses and riders, but demonic creatures that he has seen in his ecstatic state. As they are described in dramatic terms, the three plagues of fire, smoke, and sulfur come from the mouths of the horses. The fierceness and destructiveness of the animals is stressed.

As we wade through John's words about demonic influence and judgment we must be careful to remember that this is not about what will happen at the end of the age. These judgments are following upon mankind continually as they rebel again Almighty God. Don't think that the upheaval of the world is just business as usual. God is doing all He can to get the attention of mankind before it is too late to do so. Whenever we hear of the power of evil seemingly taking over certain parts of our society and world we need to understand that things are progressing according to God's plan. The Devil is not winning, however. God is just allowing him some space in order to show people how really bad a life ignoring their Creator can be. Sin always brings about a terrible price.

The Stubbornness of Sin

A third of mankind was killed by the three plagues of fire, smoke and sulfur that came out of their mouths. The power of the horses was in their mouths and in their tails; for their tails were like snakes, having heads with which they inflict injury. The rest of mankind that were not killed by these plagues still did not repent of the work of their hands; they did not stop worshiping demons, and idols of gold, silver, bronze, stone and wood–idols that cannot see or hear or walk. Nor did they repent of their murders, their magic arts, their sexual immorality or their thefts. (9:18-21)

The result of the three plagues is repeated from verse fifteen. They had received their instruction earlier and now they have carried out their murderous task.

The animals destroy both from the front and the back. The mention of snakes brings association with the demonic and John is seeing demons unleashed upon the world. The result of this trumpet is an intensification of the fifth trumpet. The power of the evil one and his forces cause disaster and destruction wherever they go.

One would expect the world to see what horrible things sin is doing and turn their hearts to the Lord, but the result is just the opposite. Hard times don't always drive people to their knees, just at Pharaoh's reaction to the plagues of Exodus. In this passage people continue their demonic practice of worshipping their man-made gods. Men in sin go deeper in sin when they refuse to yield to the call of God on their lives. Men without God hold on to the things of the world at all costs. This passage reveals one of the saddest things about human nature. It is as old as the Garden of Eden that mankind tries continually to be its own god and when it cannot it rebels and curses its fortune. How much better when God disciplines to accept it and allow it to change our behavior!

Protection for the People of God

Then I saw another mighty angel coming down from heaven. He was robed in a cloud, with a rainbow above his head; his face was like the sun, and his legs were like fiery pillars. (10:1)

At the close of chapter nine we must ask the question, "What has happened to the Church during these trumpets of judgment?" Chapters ten and eleven give us the answer to that question. 10:1-11:14 comes between the sixth and seventh trumpets just as chapter seven is placed between the sixth and seventh seals. These are times of assuring the Church of her safety in the midst of all the judgments of God on a sinful world.

John sees a great angel coming from the presence of God. Up till now little has been said about the appearance of angels because the attention was on what they did or said. But the appearance of this one is described completely. Each of the points mentioned has a connection with God the Father or with Christ, God the Son, so this angel is clearly important. The cloud and rainbow serve to enhance the flight of the angel whose face is like the sun and his feet like columns of fire. It brings memories of how the people of Israel were guided from Egypt by a column of fire.

As the third vision continues we see how secure the people of God are. The angels of God protect us and this passage shows just how big they are. We are continually in connection to our heavenly Father not only through His Spirit that lives in us, but also through the creatures He has made to protect us. The churches John was writing to were small and very limited in their power in this world. Both they and the churches that would come after them can take courage from the fact that they have not been left alone or forgotten.

Some Things We Just Can't Know

He was holding a little scroll, which lay open in his hand. He planted his right foot on the sea and his left foot on the land, and he gave a loud shout like the roar of a lion. When he shouted, the voices of the seven thunders spoke. And when the seven thunders spoke, I was about to write; but I heard a voice from heaven say, "Seal up what the seven thunders have said and do not write it down." (10:2-4)

We earlier met another strong angel who had a sealed book (5:2). Now we see this angel with an open book. He has one foot on the sea and one on the land. This shows his size and power, for in John's eyes the land and the sea were the sum total of the universe. It also shows that the power of God is just as firm on the sea as it is on the land. The little book is the gospel, the Word of God for His Church. The combination of the little book and the angel has great significance. The world despised Christians as members of a little insignificant sect that matters to no one but himself or herself. But John sees that his faith is based on the Word of God and the Word of God is in the hand of this colossal figure that spans all the earth. We see with John that the Word of God is not puny and insignificant, but supremely important. It presides over all the affairs of men.

John hears the angel cry out loudly. Seven thunders answer, but John is not allowed to tell what they say. It seems that John is being given a revelation that he is not permitted to pass on. We simply know that John had experiences that he could not communicate to others. God sometimes tells a man more than he can say, or that his generation can understand. This is hard for us. We like to solve puzzles. Here, however, we see only only God alone knows some things and the rest of us are just going to have to learn to be patient.

There is a Plan

Then the angel I had seen standing on the sea and on the land raised his right hand to heaven. And he swore by him who lives for ever and ever, who created the heavens and all that is in them, the earth and all that is in it, and the sea and all that is in it, and said, "There will be no more delay! But in the days when the seventh angel is about to sound his trumpet, the mystery of God will be accomplished, just as he announced to his servants the prophets." (10:5-7)

The mighty angel makes an oath based on the power and person of God that the justice cried for from the martyrs under the altar (6:10) will be delayed no longer. It will come to pass when the trumpet blast resumes. Since we are given this promise, there is no need to know what the thunders have uttered.

The verse does not say, "when the trumpet sounds," but "in the days when the seventh angel is about to sound his trumpet." This clearly suggests that the sounding of the trumpet is not to be thought of as a simple act; it embodies a period of time. God will keep His word to His servants of all generations.

Sometimes we feel like the world is all upside down. Sometimes it feels like evil will always reign and truth and justice will never get a chance to see the light of day. We see here a different story. It is reminiscent of Peter's words, "The Lord is not slow in keeping his promise, as some understand slowness. He is patient with you, not wanting anyone to perish, but everyone to come to repentance" (II Peter 3:9). God's timing is never early and it is never late. He will bring about what we need just when we need it.

This angel is given to us as a symbol of the fact that the Father keeps His word. He has promised us that He will be with us to the end of time and beyond. He demonstrates that He has all power and is full of grace in His plan for us. When it all comes down to basics that really is all we need to know.

The Power of the Book

Then the voice that I had heard from heaven spoke to me once more: "Go, take the scroll that lies open in the hand of the angel who is standing on the sea and on the land." So I went to the angel and asked him to give me the little scroll. He said to me, "Take it and eat it. It will turn your stomach sour, but in your mouth it will be as sweet as honey." I took the little scroll from the angel's hand and ate it. It tasted as sweet as honey in my mouth, but when I had eaten it, my stomach turned sour. Then I was told, "You must prophesy again about many peoples, nations, languages and kings." (10:8-11)

This section of the vision is clearly linked with Ezekiel 2:8-3:2. The voice that wouldn't let John write what the thunders had spoken now tells him to get the book from the mighty angel. When he does as he is instructed, the angel tells him to eat it. John was promised that it would taste sweet, but it would make his belly bitter. Ezekiel had also been instructed to eat a book that was sweet. It was significant of the fact that the Word of the Lord would be sweet, for Ezekiel was a prophet of restoration in the time of the Babylonian exile. He enjoyed sharing the sweet message of hope to the Israelite remnant.

John was also a willing prophet of the Lord, but his was "bitter-sweet" message. It was bitter because it promised hard times, woes, judgment, and punishment for the Church (by the world), but sweet because it also promised the Church a greater and final restoration in the kingdom of God.

In the eleventh verse of this chapter, Christ's last great commission to His Church is expressed in symbolic form. The little book of the gospel is to be given to other peoples, nations, tongues, and kings. As John was commissioned, so are we! The little book contains the greatest story ever told and we need to be about the task of taking its good news to everyone, everywhere.

The Church is in Good Hands

I was given a reed like a measuring rod and was told, "Go and measure the temple of God and the altar, and count the worshipers there. But exclude the outer court; do not measure it, because it has been given to the Gentiles. They will trample on the holy city for 42 months. (11:1-2)

As a follow-up to eating the little book, John is instructed to measure the part of the temple where worship is being carried on. He is to leave out of his measurements the outer part of the temple where the Gentiles would meet. It is not measured because it is the place where those who are outside the kingdom of God (the Church) live. John is telling us that the Church will be preserved, but not those who are outside its protection. The body of Christ will no doubt be trampled underfoot, but not destroyed. The safety of the Church is not guaranteed physically, but spiritually. The Church being measured brings across the same idea as the Church being sealed in chapter seven.

The forty-two months are three and a half years. This length of time had, by John's time, become a symbol of a time period for the triumph of evil. It is a broken seven—which is the number of perfection. What it means to us is that it is possible for persecution to be very severe and may even lead to death for the Christian, but it is not permanent. The lives of those who belong to the Church are preserved in Christ.

The old song says, "This world is not my home, I'm only passing through…" Our reward is not here, but on the other side. Let's never forget that. The days may sometimes seem dark and pressures mount as we live in stressful situations, but we are not alone. We are sealed, measured, and secure in the love of God. He has never failed us and never will.

Called to be a Witness

And I will give power to my two witnesses, and they will prophesy for 1,260 days, clothed in sackcloth." These are the two olive trees and the two lampstands that stand before the Lord of the earth. (11:3-4)

John plays upon a repeated theme when he speaks of "forty-two months," "1260 days," "three and a half years," "three and a half days," and in 12:14 "time, times, and half a time." They all mean the same thing. It is the symbol of the broken seven again. It is a reflection of Daniel 7:25 and 12:7, where the prophet speaks of the persecution of the saints. It is also interesting to note that the Israelites had forty-two encampments in the wilderness (Numbers 33:5ff). The important thing to remember is that John is speaking of an indefinite period of time where evil seems to have the upper hand.

Two witnesses now appear. Speculation of these two characters has ranged from Moses and Elijah, to Elijah and Elisha, Elijah and Enoch, the Law and the Prophets, the Law and Gospel, and the Old and New Testaments. There is no end of these imaginative ideas. But if we look at the symbolism John has already used we see that these witnesses are not two literal men, but are symbols of the collective people of God. Chapter 4:4 referred to the combined groups of the saints of all ages, first associated with Judaism and then with Christianity. In heaven the redeemed will wear white robes and golden crowns, but here on earth they are dressed in sackcloth. Ours is to be a humble existence. There is a degree of mourning and penitence in the Christian life. The witnesses are also called olive trees and lampstands. That the Church is called lampstands was revealed back in chapter one. The olive oil is a reminder of the Church's mission to give the gospel (oil) to a world that is hurting and in the dark.

The Church in Power

If anyone tries to harm them, fire comes from their mouths and devours their enemies. This is how anyone who wants to harm them must die. These men have power to shut up the sky so that it will not rain during the time they are prophesying; and they have power to turn the waters into blood and to strike the earth with every kind of plague as often as they want. (11:5-6)

A fire that comes out of their mouths protects the witnesses. Certainly the word of the faithful Christian who exalts his Lord is a consuming fire. Anyone who would harm God's own will face His fiery wrath.

In the case of these witnesses having power to control nature and bring plagues, it may well be John's point to say that the enacting of the Church in its duty is how judgments of God are brought to pass in our wicked world. Those who oppose the gospel witness will ultimately be destroyed and the commitment of God's people to pray and believe will always have results of catastrophic effect on the world. The results may not always be physical, but God's army shakes the dark regions through spiritual warfare.

It certainly is easier to make these witnesses out to be real individuals and join in on the speculation about who they are. However, John is speaking about principles and is showing the witness of the Church of Jesus Christ. Through the power of the Spirit the Church will always have power to do the impossible. Judgment and blessing belong to the Lord alone.

We like to believe the stories of the Bible miracles, but often regulate them to another time and place alone. God's power has not diminished, however. What He has done in another time He can do now. What He has done in another place He can do here. We can trust Him for today's needs.

There Will Be Dark Days

Now when they have finished their testimony, the beast that comes up from the Abyss will attack them, and overpower and kill them. (11:7)

The reality of the effectiveness of the witnesses is not exactly encouraging. There is no mention of anyone who believes the gospel and is converted as a result of their message. The best that can be said for their ministry is that they made life miserable for earth's population. They do fully accomplish their task however. John is always reflecting on the persecution of God's people and the resulting punishment upon those who do the persecuting. When their job is over, the beast (symbol of the forces of evil) from the pit overcomes them and brings about their deaths. The message that John is trying to get across is that when Christ's followers have fulfilled their purpose they are removed from the conflict. This is a promise to the Church of all generations. We are to do the job Christ has called us to do and we will not be stopped until it is finished, even if all the forces of hell are thrown against us. But once our mission is complete, the Lord will release us from the battle.

God is always faithful to His own. He knows how much we can endure and knows when it is time to call us home. That's why Christians have no fear from what the world can throw at them. When Jesus said, "I am going to prepare a place for you…" (John 14:3) we can believe His words and know that He will bring us to that place at just the right time. There is no reason to worry about the future. He has things well under control. Feel like the pressure is great? Feel the fire getting hotter? Then you are experiencing what Christians have for centuries. Be of good cheer, however. We are overcomers through Christ!

Resurrection Power

Their bodies will lie in the street of the great city, which is figuratively called Sodom and Egypt, where also their Lord was crucified. For three and a half days men from every people, tribe, language and nation will gaze on their bodies and refuse them burial. The inhabitants of the earth will gloat over them and will celebrate by sending each other gifts, because these two prophets had tormented those who live on the earth. But after the three and a half days a breath of life from God entered them, and they stood on their feet, and terror struck those who saw them. (11:8-11)

After the faithful are slain the world rejoices. It considers the fallen Church a laughingstock and forever dead. Whenever men of faith fall they are ridiculed mercilessly by those who count Christianity as just another useless religion. Even when they have been faithful Christians have been slain by the millions down through the centuries and their oppressors have gloated over their victory. When the voice of condemnation is silenced, the conscience for a time grows quiet. Sodom and Egypt are symbols of our world that killed our Lord. All now seems to be going the way of the evil one, but the end is not yet.

The good news of the gospel, however, is that the dead come back to life. History has many times seen the Church of the edge of being destroyed, but it always rises from where it has fallen. Each time that the Church regains her strength and marches into battle, amazement and fear fall upon her enemies.

The Apostle Paul knew this fact to be true when he penned, "Therefore God exalted him to the highest place and gave him the name that is above every name, that at the name of Jesus every knee should bow, in heaven and on earth and under the earth, and every tongue confess that Jesus Christ is Lord, to the glory of God the Father" (Philippians 2:9-11). It's true that we may get knocked down at times, but we who are in Christ will be standing when the last bell rings.

In the End, We Win!

Then they heard a loud voice from heaven saying to them, "Come up here." And they went up to heaven in a cloud, while their enemies looked on. At that very hour there was a severe earthquake and a tenth of the city collapsed. Seven thousand people were killed in the earthquake, and the survivors were terrified and gave glory to the God of heaven. The second woe has passed; the third woe is coming soon. The seventh angel sounded his trumpet, and there were loud voices in heaven, which said: "The kingdom of the world has become the kingdom of our Lord and of his Christ, and he will reign for ever and ever." (11:12-15)

John then moves to the final great event of history, which is when the Church is taken up out of the world. The Church hears the call from above and rises to its reward in full view of her enemies. Those who remain are filled with fear to the point that even they will begin to glorify God. It is a picture of the words of the Apostle Paul, "And having disarmed the powers and authorities, he made a public spectacle of them, triumphing over them by the cross" (Colossian 2:15). But it is too late for the unrepentant. The third and final "woe" of God's judgment is upon them.

It has been a long interval since the sixth angel blew his trumpet, but now the seventh horn sounds. The first thing that happens is not judgment, but a chorus of the heavenly hosts proclaiming the Lordship and Kingdom of Christ. Imagine the terror of hearing this powerful proclamation when the inhabitants of the sinful world have scoffed at the idea for so long. However, for the Christian this will be the happiest day that we could ever think about.

We who believe in Christ are often scoffed at and ridiculed either to our face or behind our backs because of our faith. It may sometimes be difficult to stand strong, but be of good cheer. In the end, we win – and the winning is worth the wait!

Back to the Praise Party

And the twenty-four elders, who were seated on their thrones before God, fell on their faces and worshiped God, saying: "We give thanks to you, Lord God Almighty, the One who is and who was, because you have taken your great power and have begun to reign. The nations were angry; and your wrath has come. The time has come for judging the dead, and for rewarding your servants the prophets and your saints and those who reverence your name, both small and great—and for destroying those who destroy the earth." Then God's temple in heaven was opened, and within his temple was seen the ark of his covenant. And there came flashes of lightning, rumblings, peals of thunder, an earthquake and a great hailstorm. (11:16-19)

The last time that the twenty-four elders were mentioned was between the sixth and seventh seals (7:11). Again they fall before the throne and worship as they give a brief account of their experience on earth. They announce the end. The time of judgment has come as well as the time for the rewarding of the saints and the eternal destruction of the lost.

At this point we see a temple in heaven and we can peer into the presence of God, which is symbolized by the Ark of the Covenant. The Ark was always the symbol of God's presence in the Old Testament. The scene is one of complete victory. The wicked are destroyed, the Kingdom of God is established on earth, and God rules in the presence of His people under the new covenant. The Church is no longer the Church *militant*, but the Church *triumphant* and eternity is underway.

This scene is almost like fireworks that are going off. It is the view of a celebration that is taking place in heaven continually. It was going on during John's day, it is going on now, and it will be going on throughout eternity. In the presence of the Lord there is continual praise and thanksgiving being offered to God. The Lamb has overcome. It is an ever-present reality!

The Fourth Vision: Revelation 12:1-14:20

We now go from the end of time at the end of chapter eleven, back to the beginning once again—just as we did in the previous visions. Chapters 12-13 show what is happening in the secular world during the present age. Chapter 14 shows what is happening in the heavenly realm during the same time.

1. The woman represents the people of God of all ages. In response to their need Jesus is born into the world. The dragon (Satan) tries to kill Him, but He is protected until He returns to heaven. (12:1-16)
2. There is an inset in the story. This tells of the removal of Satan and his followers from heaven. It is not to be understood in chronological order. He is defeated and thrown down to the earth and persecutes the Church, which is protected by God for as long as his time remains. (12:7-13:1)
3. Satan enlists some help. He gives power to the beast. The beast is to be understood as any national power that would take upon itself the role of lordship over men. It could be Rome, Greece, France, Germany, Japan, the USSR, Iraq, or the USA. It is any government, empowered by Satan that tries to defeat the ultimate plan of God. He only has the time of the Church-age to operate however. (13:2-10)
4. Satan rallies another ally. A second beast comes into being. This is understood as a religious force in the world, supported by the state (the first beast), empowered by Satan (the dragon). (13:11-15)
5. To refuse to give allegiance to the state (beast 1) or the state religion (beast 2) means death. To show allegiance, one must give full-hearted devotion to the cause. This is known as

receiving a "mark." The symbol for the mark is 666. Just as the people of God have been "sealed" (8:1–5), or "measured" (11:1–2), the people that are not on God's side have a "mark." Everyone has one mark or the other. (13:16–18)

6. The 144,000 represent the Church, or "the sealed" of God. A scene of judgment is presented. The sealed will be saved. The marked will be lost. There is a blessing given to those who die in the Lord for their reward is secure. (14:1–13)

7. The earth is harvested. First, the Church (the sealed) is gathered by Jesus to its eternal reward. Next, the lost world (the marked) is gathered by an angel who takes them to destruction. The scene is graphic and the destruction of the lost is complete. (14:14–20)

A New View of the Christmas Story

A great and wondrous sign appeared in heaven: a woman clothed with the sun, with the moon under her feet and a crown of twelve stars on her head. She was pregnant and cried out in pain as she was about to give birth. (12:1-2)

As we enter into chapter twelve we begin the fourth of the seven visions, telling the story of the conflict between the Church of Jesus Christ and Satan and his forces. We see a spiritual battle going on that has physical repercussions.

We now go from the end of time at the end of chapter eleven, back to the beginning once again—just as we did at the start of the previous visions. Chapters twelve through fourteen contain one vision, which is like a cosmic drama. Chapters twelve and thirteen pull back the curtain and let mankind witness a behind-the-scenes view of what is happening in the evil world during this present age.

It is the first time in this book that a woman has depicted the Church (the people of God of all times—the true Israel). She is a symbol for the Church universal. The "woman clothed with the sun" is in direct contrast to the "great prostitute" (17:1). The fact that she has twelve stars as a crown on her head gives more evidence that she is indeed the Church, for twelve is a symbol for organized religion throughout this book and we are told in 1:20 that the stars are the "angels" or "leaders" of the churches.

The woman (the family of God) is about to give birth and is going through labor pains. There were many devout souls before the coming of Christ who waited and anticipated the Messiah's arrival. We see here the unfolding of God's plan for our redemption. This is the Christmas story in apocalyptic form.

The Enemy of the King

Then another sign appeared in heaven: an enormous red dragon with seven heads and ten horns and seven crowns on his heads. His tail swept a third of the stars out of the sky and flung them to the earth. The dragon stood in front of the woman who was about to give birth, so that he might devour her child the moment it was born. (12:3-4)

As John plays out this drama, he sees another amazing sight. The dragon he sees is Satan, who is the prince of this world. He is described as being red with the symbol of seven heads, seven crowns, and seven horns. The red stands for the murderous way that he destroys and we will also see that the great prostitute is clothed in scarlet and red is also the color of the beast she sits on (17:1). The number seven again represents the symbol of perfection, but this time the perfection has a negative connotation. It stands for perfect vileness, or the perfection of evil. The number ten brings about the idea of completeness for the kingdoms of the world have all been under the effects of Satan from the beginning. From the Garden of Eden all the way to the present day, there is not a place anywhere that has not been touched by the stench of sin.

The main thrust of these verses is that the dragon is waiting to kill the child of the woman when he is born. This child is a direct reference to Jesus. The evil one has been trying to destroy the Christ from the time that He came into the world; first through Herod's massacre and later through temptations and tests. He tried to destroy the Christ just like he tries to destroy all who belong to Him. The Father has a plan for His Son, however, as He does for us and His plans never fail.

We don't need to fear the threats and plots of the enemy. We can take comfort that God always makes a way for His own and we that in Christ are His!

The Resurrection is Coming

She gave birth to a son, a male child, who will rule all the nations with an iron scepter. And her child was snatched up to God and to his throne. The woman fled into the desert to a place prepared for her by God, where she might be taken care of for 1,260 days. (12:5-6)

The male child that is born (Jesus) is going to rule the nations with an iron scepter. This is a direct allusion to Psalm 2:9. Not only was Jesus rescued from Satan at the time of His birth, but was protected throughout His ministry. After the crucifixion and the resurrection He ascended back to heaven. This little story that John tells is the gospel in a nutshell. It begins with Christmas and goes through the ascension and even shows what happens to the Church following Christ's bodily departure. In a style of writing that most are not quite used to in our time, John preaches the "Good News" of the Kingdom!

By this simple story John is relating the defeat of Satan. These are encouraging words to the infant Church. Just as the evil one tried to destroy the Christ, but was unsuccessful, the Church can take great comfort in the fact that they will be overcomers as well. As Christ was lifted up, so will the Church one day be lifted up to the glory of the Father!

Along with this thought is the fact that the woman's place was prepared by God. She was not forgotten after the Messiah had ascended to heaven. God will care for her throughout the entire history of this age (the 1260 days). The wilderness life lasts through the whole Christian era. We should never forget that we are who are the redeemed are to be strangers here (I Peter 1:1), but even as strangers we abide under the shelter of the Almighty (Psalm 91:1). Our hope is not in what happens in this world but in the resurrection!

Days of Testing

And there was war in heaven. Michael and his angels fought against the dragon, and the dragon and his angels fought back. But he was not strong enough, and they lost their place in heaven. The great dragon was hurled down–that ancient serpent called the devil, or Satan, who leads the whole world astray. He was hurled to the earth, and his angels with him. Then I heard a loud voice in heaven say: "Now have come the salvation and the power and the kingdom of our God, and the authority of his Christ. For the accuser of our brothers, who accuses them before our God day and night, has been hurled down. They overcame him by the blood of the Lamb and by the word of their testimony; they did not love their lives so much as to shrink from death. Therefore rejoice, you heavens and you who dwell in them! But woe to the earth and the sea, because the devil has gone down to you! He is filled with fury, because he knows that his time is short." (12:7-12)

This section of scripture is like an inset view of a map. We see a behind-the-scenes look at a heavenly battle. The story is told of how Satan and his demons lost their place in heaven. It is told in retrospect. A great battle took place and the angels of Michael defeat the angels of Satan and he is forever cast out of the rewards of eternity.

John uses a bit of poetry to make his proclamation of the victory of right over wrong. The Church continues to be victorious through the blood of the Lamb. Satan may destroy the bodies of Christians, but when that happens, like their Lord they are caught up to be with their Father. It is a message that the Church can rejoice about.

The scene being described here is the totality of the church age. It is an age of conflict even though the final outcome has already been decided. The Church will continually be oppressed and the battle will rage on against the powers of darkness until Jesus comes again. This is a testing time. It is a preparation time for the world to come. It is a time that God has ordained our eternal good.

Times of Protection

When the dragon saw that he had been hurled to the earth, he pursued the woman who had given birth to the male child. The woman was given the two wings of a great eagle, so that she might fly to the place prepared for her in the desert, where she would be taken care of for a time, times and half a time, out of the serpent's reach. Then from his mouth the serpent spewed water like a river, to overtake the woman and sweep her away with the torrent. But the earth helped the woman by opening its mouth and swallowing the river that the dragon had spewed out of his mouth. Then the dragon was enraged at the woman and went off to make war against the rest of her offspring–those who obey God's commandments and hold to the testimony of Jesus. (12:13-17)

The persecution of the Church is the result of the defeat of Satan in his attempt to destroy the Christ. He has lost power in heaven and is imprisoned on the planet, so he makes war with anyone resembling his conqueror. He is trying to punish the Church, but the Church is protected from him.

John uses several images here that cannot be taken literally. His words are given for inspiration, not necessarily for information. Naturally, the Church does not fly on eagles wings, but is given a way to escape by the Master. She is protected for the duration of the Church age.

We must remember the terms "time, times, and half a time," "three and a half years," "three and a half days," and "1260 days" all mean the same thing. It is referring to the entire Church age. The Church will always be protected from the reach of Satan as she relies on the One who has defeated him.

It would be nice to think that all would be rosy and well for all who put their trust in Christ. However, time and experience, as well as the Word of God, show that this is just not true. In this world we will have trouble, but it is meant to cause us to lean that much more on the Lord and trust His strength to get us through. We learn that when we are weak, He truly is our sustaining power.

When Men Try to Become Gods...

And the dragon stood on the shore of the sea. And I saw a beast coming out of the sea. He had ten horns and seven heads, with ten crowns on his horns, and on each head a blasphemous name. (13:1)

Since the sea was a frightening thing to many of the people of John's time, it is only natural that the comrade of the dragon should come from the murky depths of the sea. It is easy to tell that the beast is evil for it resembles the description that we have been given of the dragon. They both have seven heads and ten horns. The dragon is spiritual evil, but the beast from the sea represents a tangible force of evil in the world. One is unseen, but the other acts visibly to do the bidding of its evil counterpart.

Though the dragon is present behind the scenes, the beast takes the spotlight and the world is affected by it. We can be sure that the beast is royalty because of the crown on his horns, but it is an evil royalty. Its blasphemy is so strong that it is written upon is heads. Any national power of John's day or ours, who would take upon itself the rightful place of Lordship over men, would fit into the category of the beast. The beast is not a person or any particular nationality (though it seems clear from the context that John sees it in his day as Rome); it is a symbol of spiritual wickedness in high places of human power.

The Roman Emperor Nero even went so far as to have the words *The Savior of the World* printed on his coins. Certainly this is blasphemy! Rome, Babylon, Berlin, Moscow, Washington D.C., or any government that usurps the power of the Almighty by exalting its own or that which is evil, fits into the image of the beast that John is describing here. The first sin is of man trying to be a god. The last sins will be no different.

Tools of the Enemy

The beast I saw resembled a leopard, but had feet like those of a bear and a mouth like that of a lion. The dragon gave the beast his power and his throne and great authority. (13:2)

We have to understand that John is not expecting his readers to take the picture of this beast literally, but symbolically. The description of the beast is meant to portray the horrible. He is not so concerned with the fact that the beast has seven heads but only one mouth. These are images of evil taking a physical form. The importance of the verse is seen in the fact that Satan is at the root of this power and he has given liberty for the beast to do evil. This beast is a formidable enemy. Though Satan has already been defeated, the Christian should not be deceived into thinking that he no longer has any power. Just as a drowning individual may pull a rescuer down with him, Satan is grasping at straws through the power given to the beast.

We have watched many nations take the role of the beast. Nations that thrive on corrupt governments, deceitful leaders, and the oppression of righteousness assume the image of the beast. For the Christian, there can only be one king. There is only one highway of holiness (Isaiah 35:8) and one Lord of the highway. Satan will do all he can to empower those nations who reject the direction of the Almighty.

Just look around our world today. Look at all the unrest, riots, and unstable economies as a result of corruption and shady deals. Such governments are tools of the dragon and are the beast for our time. The world will always have the wicked until the end, but God has promised He would be around for that long also—and aren't we glad!

A Government of Evil

One of the heads of the beast seemed to have had a fatal wound, but the fatal wound had been healed. The whole world was astonished and followed the beast. (13:3)

Because John makes the statement that one of the beast's heads was mortally wounded, it is easy to see how this could be attributed to Rome. It has been said that not only did the seven heads of the beast symbolize the seven hills of Rome, but also seven emperors. After Augustus, the first Roman emperor, there were seven other major rulers: Tiberius (A.D 14-37), Caligula (A.D. 37-41), Claudius (A.D. 41-54), Nero (A.D. 55-68), Vespasian (A.D. 69-79), Titus (A.D. 79-81, and Domitian (81-96). Galba, Otho, and Vitellius also sat on the throne during the year A.D. 69, but these are not considered to be significant as rulers. It makes perfect sense for people of the first century to realize that one of the emperors could die and then the beast could continue right on as though it had been healed. Another emperor would simply take his place. No doubt it would be an amazing thing to see how evil could remain so constant a force, even through a change in leadership—but such is the partner of Satan.

So many people have tried to make this into something that should appear on a tabloid stand. It doesn't help the cause of Christ to speculate and put the name of men in the place of the beast. Such wild accusations have made the Church look foolish down through the centuries. The beast, at least for John, is the nation of Rome and its rulers. It is also any nation that turns its back on God and John is warning the people of his generation and all generations that if we leave God out of our lives and our governments then we join partnership with the enemy of our souls.

Leadership Empowered By the Enemy

Men worshiped the dragon because he had given authority to the beast, and they also worshiped the beast and asked, "Who is like the beast? Who can make war against him?" The beast was given a mouth to utter proud words and blasphemies and to exercise his authority for forty-two months. (13:4-5)

As men blindly follow the leading of a pagan government, they find themselves in league with the devil. In John's day men were forced to worship the emperor as though he were God. This brings glory to Satan, who is still smarting over his defeat at the cross. Oftentimes we look at our own society and wonder who can make a difference. We wonder who could ever overcome the powers that are in place. Who can fight city hall? The whole picture of this powerful dragon and the beast seem too much to fight against. Man must always choose the one that will be his god and then live with the consequences.

The idea that the beast "was *given* a mouth" (italics mine) lets us know that he has no power on his own. His strength comes from the evil one. But even with such power placed upon him the Church of Jesus Christ can recognize that God is still in control of the scene, for He has limited the scope of this evil pair's activity.

They can only have authority for "forty-two months." Satan will have the time of this earthly existence to tempt, kill, and deceive through whatever means he may try, but there is coming a day when his time will be up. As we have seen on various earlier occasions, the forty-two month period is another way of describing the Church age. We are living in the forty-two month period now, just as John was. It is a very general term, not one of specific length. The world will be in the forty-two month period until Jesus comes again.

There is no Cheap Grace

He opened his mouth to blaspheme God, and to slander his name and his dwelling place and those who live in heaven. He was given power to make war against the saints and to conquer them. And he was given authority over every tribe, people, language and nation. All inhabitants of the earth will worship the beast—all whose names have not been written in the book of life belonging to the Lamb that was slain from the creation of the world. He who has an ear, let him hear. If anyone is to go into captivity, into captivity he will go. If anyone is to be killed with the sword, with the sword he will be killed. This calls for patient endurance and faithfulness on the part of the saints. (13:6-10)

The beast goes on a rampage. The forces of evil have always blasphemed and slandered the name and things of God. To this day there are those who scoff at the ideas of heaven and hell or at the fact that there is truly a God at all—and many times there have been beast-like governments that have backed such ideas.

Through the dark period of history there have been times when Christians have fallen victim to the satanic prodding of men in high places. Bodies have been slain and some who have once testified to be followers of Christ have fallen away. There is not a nation, race, language, or tribe anywhere on the face of the planet that has not been affected by the dragon and the beast. Only those who have been sealed by the seal of God, those who have their names written in the book of life, and those who have been washed in the blood of the Lamb will not worship what is evil. Men will sell their souls and their votes for money, comfort, and power, but those who truly belong to Christ will cling to what is right at all costs. This is the very reason why there are so many who begin the walk with Christ who do not finish it. Our Lord freely gives grace, but it is not cheap. There is a price that is sometime very dear to be paid to walk in faith.

The Danger of False Beliefs

Then I saw another beast, coming out of the earth. He had two horns like a lamb, but he spoke like a dragon. He exercised all the authority of the first beast on his behalf, and made the earth and its inhabitants worship the first beast, whose fatal wound had been healed. And he performed great and miraculous signs, even causing fire to come down from heaven to earth in full view of men. (13:11-13)

This first beast is not alone. He has a henchman to help him do his dastardly deeds. A second beast comes out of the earth instead of the sea as the first one did. This makes the second beast less fearsome than the first beast.

Note that there are just two horns on the second beast as compared with ten on the first. A strong line of thought implies that this second beast represents the priesthood, or an organized religion that casts its lot with an evil government as a false religion. The result is that instead of sharing the gospel as true religion should, this beast speaks like the dragon that it follows.

This beast has all the backing and power of the first beast. In other words, the state religion has the full blessing and support of the state. The purpose of the second beast is to get the people of the earth to worship the first beast.

How often governments have tried to get a hold on people's spiritual hunger and have promised to fill that void with what man can produce through his united efforts. It was happening in John's day, it was happening in Nazi Germany, it was happening in the communistic Soviet Union, and it is still happening today in Islamic countries throughout the world. Wherever governments use religion to strangle people we see this happening.

This is why it is so vital that we know what we believe and that our doctrine is pure. False religion has always been one of the devil's strongest tools.

Getting the Cart Before the Horse

Because of the signs he was given power to do on behalf of the first beast, he deceived the inhabitants of the earth. He ordered them to set up an image in honor of the beast who was wounded by the sword and yet lived. He was given power to give breath to the image of the first beast, so that it could speak and cause all who refused to worship the image to be killed. (13:14-15)

Through subtlety and craftiness, organized religion has used the ignorance of men to gain victims to their deadly game. In John's day there were many sorcerers and magicians who used deception to win over the unsuspecting masses. In our own day charlatans have used trickery to fake healings, ecstatic experiences, and visions. John sees these tools used to bring glory to the state, which in his time is controlled by the devil.

Emperor worship became part of the state religion and all were expected to pay homage to the king. The image of Caesar was to be literally worshipped and no one was to be excluded. Christians had to make a choice. Christians always have to make a choice. A man can only truly serve and worship one God.

With the state religion being the mouthpiece for the state government, a lot of pressure was placed on all citizens to conform to the wishes of the empire and worship the image of the emperor. To refuse meant certain death. No longer could people straddle the fence as to where their loyalties would lie.

We should treasure our nations as gifts from God, but we must always keep in perspective that it is He who rules over the countries as well as over the hearts of men. When we leave Him out, we leave out the source of the freedoms we cherish. Belief, however, must be left to the individual for when governments get control of religion it usually turns sour and into a tool for the beast.

The Danger of the Mark

He also forced everyone, small and great, rich and poor, free and slave, to receive a mark on his right hand or on his forehead, so that no one could buy or sell unless he had the mark, which is the name of the beast or the number of his name. This calls for wisdom. If anyone has insight, let him calculate the number of the beast, for it is man's number. His number is 666. (13:16-18)

Like other parts of this book, a lot of speculation has been displayed as to what the mark is, how it is to be given, and when it is to be. We could give opinions endlessly. In keeping with the style of writing we have been investigating, and with the context of the overall flow of the book, however, there seems only one plausible answer. The mark is a symbol, not a literal stamp.

666 is the number for evil in triplicate. Six is the number of imperfection. Seven is the number of perfection. 666 will never be seven. It is always short of the mark and the definition of "sin" (Greek—*hamartia*) is "missing the mark." To choose the mark of the beast is to settle for less than the perfect walk in Christ. By choosing to burn incense to Caesar and proclaiming him "Lord" one aligned himself with the way of the dragon and the two beasts. In John's day, going the way of the state edicts was the only way to remain free and able to do business. This is the meaning of the mark of the beast.

We can look for someone to put a literal stamp on our heads or hands and miss the message that the scripture is trying to get across. Christianity has never been about what we do or don't do. It is, and always has been about the state of our devotion—the state of our hearts. It is about belief or unbelief. If we have not accepted Jesus Christ as the Lord and Savior of our lives, the mark of the beast is already upon us.

The Redeemed Shine Through

Then I looked, and there before me was the Lamb, standing on Mount Zion, and with him 144,000 who had his name and his Father's name written on their foreheads. (14:1)

As in chapters seven and ten, we now have another interlude of hope as the Church is reminded that even though it may have a rough way to go in this world and that there will be many who will not be faithful, there is coming a day of celebration and rejoicing because the victory has already been determined.

John sees the events of the ages as if they had already taken place. We are reminded that God is not bound by time and that he knows all things. He can reveal these events to whomever He chooses and in this case the final victory is shown to John. This is a message of hope and courage to suffering Christians. Great pressure is on them in this world, but someday they will join the singing around the throne of God that is already going on. Not even the dragon or his beasts can stop that!

As we have seen before, the 144,000 are the saints who have been redeemed. As the 144,000 had been sealed, now we see 144,000 saved. Not one has been lost. God always takes care of those who belong to Him. They are the Church universal and they stand in stark contrast to all the people who have worshipped the beast and have received its stamp on their lives. Satan has embedded his mark on his followers and the Holy One has placed His seal on those who belong to Him. Everyone fits into one of these categories.

This first part of chapter fourteen needs to always be paired with the last part of chapter thirteen. The mark of the beast and the sealing of the redeemed show which side we are on.

The New Song

And I heard a sound from heaven like the roar of rushing waters and like a loud peal of thunder. The sound I heard was like that of harpists playing their harps. And they sang a new song before the throne and before the four living creatures and the elders. No one could learn the song except the 144,000 who had been redeemed from the earth. (14:2-3)

Out of heaven John hears singing and the playing of harps. This is no small musical band, but a host of the angels who sing and play what seems to be a new song of the story of redemption. Their audience is made up of the four living creatures (symbol for all of creation), the twenty-four elders (symbol for the Old Testament and the New Testament people of God), and the Holy One who sits upon the throne, but only the 144,000 were able to learn the words. These are the saints who were ready and waiting for the return of the Lord Jesus. They are the only ones who could learn the song because they are the only ones who had experienced redemption.

We should never take lightly the great gift that salvation actually is. Those of us who were raised in the church have the greatest danger here. When all we have known is the community of grace it is hard to imagine life outside of it. But for those who have been transformed from lives of deep sin there seems to be a deeper appreciation for what has happened in their lives. Perhaps it would pay us all to consider more deeply how important salvation is. Without this work of grace we would not only be poorer in experience, but lost in eternity.

We should pray that God will help all of us to sing the "new song" of the redeemed and to sing it enthusiastically. The angels can't do it; it is our job. We who are the blessed and delivered will want to be in good voice when we are called to lead the praise parade.

The Marks of the Redeemed

These are those who did not defile themselves with women, for they kept themselves pure. They follow the Lamb wherever he goes. They were purchased from among men and offered as firstfruits to God and the Lamb. No lie was found in their mouths; they are blameless. (14:4-5)

The people of God are described in terms of purity and honesty, and are in step with the Master as He has led them throughout their lives. They have the seal of God and this celebration is part of their reward for refusing to worship the beast. They are the "firstfruits," a sacrifice offered up to God because they remained faithful in spite of all that the evil trinity (the dragon and the two beasts) could do to them. They remained faithful to their deaths.

This is a challenge for all who have spending eternity with the Lord as a goal. It does make a difference how we live. We have been given the responsibility to lead holy lives not only as a witness to the world, but also as a tribute to the God we serve. When we become so much like the world with our entertainments, language, and general activities that even the world can't tell who we are, then we shame our Lord. If we want to be witnesses to Christ we must make sure that our lifestyles help the world see that there is a difference between those who merely testify to having religion and those who have the genuine article.

Keeping ourselves pure, honest, and blameless holds a great deal of appeal to our King. He wants to present us to Himself as a glorious Church, free from impurity (Ephesians 5:27) and He will settle for nothing less. As Christ was the firstfruit to rise from the dead, all who inherit eternal life are firstfruits of the redeemed. Though temptations abound in this old sinful world, the grace of Christ is sufficient to sustain us holy unto the Lord.

Give Him the Glory

Then I saw another angel flying in midair, and he had the eternal gospel to proclaim to those who live on the earth–to every nation, tribe, language and people. He said in a loud voice, "Fear God and give him glory, because the hour of his judgment has come. Worship him who made the heavens, the earth, the sea and the springs of water." (14:6-7)

The coming verses begin a pronouncement by angels of what is to come concerning the wrath of God upon the world that has rejected the preaching of the gospel. The first three angels are airborne and have a message for all to hear.

The first angel calls for the worship and adoration of God. The end is upon them and men are urged to worship the Creator, even though some of them have chosen not to serve Him at this time.

This is good advice for anyone, anytime. If we would only learn to fear God and give Him glory we would find that most of life's problems would shrink in size and possibly even vanish. When our praise is up to date our whole outlook on life is affected and it is noticed not only by the Lord, but also by people who are around us. It's more than a matter of positive thinking; it is anointed living because God inhabits the praises of His people.

This angel who has the gospel to proclaim is carrying out the same job that we have—taking the good news of Christ to all parts of the globe and to every people group. It is imperative that we take this seriously because it is true that judgment is coming and we want to be part of the solution, not part of the problem. There is no higher mission than to make Christ-like disciples in the nations of the earth.

What is the Focus of Your Life?

A second angel followed and said, "Fallen! Fallen is Babylon the Great, which made all the nations drink the maddening wine of her adulteries." (14:8)

A second angel makes the proclamation that Babylon has fallen. No doubt for John this would be the Roman Empire, which was the symbol for the unbelieving world.

Just as the first angel carried the news of the gospel of hope, this angel specifies the judgment of God. We should understand that even though we serve a God of limitless love, He is also a God of impeccable justice. To allow this "Babylon" to escape without penalty would not be love, but complete injustice.

The "adulteries" point to a people who have had other lovers than the Lord Jesus. Whenever people make sports, music, work, money, fame, and other attractions of this world take the place of highest devotion in their lives, then they are guilty of committing adultery against the King of Love. We were made to give God glory and to devote our lives to Him.

Notice that the angel refers to the "falling" of Babylon in the present tense. That's because the judgment of God is not a one-time event, but continues throughout the ages. This is not a picture of the end, but a pronouncement of the inevitable for any group of people or individuals who lead others away from the throne of grace. It is sad for anyone to be lost, but especially tragic for those who are led astray by those who should know better. That is the judgment given here. People are always watching and we should always be pointing them to the empty tomb.

Patience is a Virtue

A third angel followed them and said in a loud voice: "If anyone worships the beast and his image and receives his mark on the forehead or on the hand, he, too, will drink of the wine of God's fury, which has been poured full strength into the cup of his wrath. He will be tormented with burning sulfur in the presence of the holy angels and of the Lamb. And the smoke of their torment rises for ever and ever. There is no rest day or night for those who worship the beast and his image, or for anyone who receives the mark of his name." This calls for patient endurance on the part of the saints who obey God's commandments and remain faithful to Jesus. (14:9-11)

The third angel gives out a warning to anyone who would be swayed by the beast and receives the mark of evil upon his or her life. Even though they may not be actively worshipping, if they have received his mark they will join in his punishment. God's wrath will be poured out on them and they will be tormented without relief through the ages.

The reference to fire and brimstone brings to mind the Old Testament story of Sodom and Gomorrah, which received a fiery judgment. It is meant to show the severity of God's hand. They will suffer punishment surrounded by observers—the holy angels and the Son of God. They had refused to walk with Him in life, but He will be with them in death as their jailer.

The picture is one of eternal despair, but there is also a reminder for the saints to be patient. In light of the eternal consequences, it is better to keep faith in Jesus and follow God than face His wrath in the time of judgment. Because there is often so much evil continually on our televisions, in our newspapers, and even in our own neighborhoods we may wonder if there is any hope for real change. John lets us know that there is—if we will just remain faithful to Christ. We know He will remain faithful to us and will reward us in due time.

The Blessed Dead

Then I heard a voice from heaven say, "Write: Blessed are the dead who die in the Lord from now on." "Yes," says the Spirit, "they will rest from their labor, for their deeds will follow them." I looked, and there before me was a white cloud, and seated on the cloud was one "like a son of man" with a crown of gold on his head and a sharp sickle in his hand. (14:13-14)

John is then given a message to write down. If this book had no other purpose but to comfort the bereaved, this one verse would make it priceless. It is one of the greatest beatitudes in the Bible (and one of seven in this book) for it gives us hope for those who have fallen asleep in Christ. It is the Holy Spirit of God Himself who makes the promise that rest is available for the weary and also the promise that their works will continue with them in the next life. As we have served the Lord here, we will serve Him there.

Heaven is not a place of idleness. The labors that we have begun for Christ here will be perfected in the next life. This is one of the reasons Christians need to learn to be productive now. All we are doing here is to lay the groundwork for our service in heaven for eternity. We will be involved in labors of love and joy, happily perfecting what we fall short of finishing in this world. All painful toil will be gone, but our works will carry on.

This final section of this vision gives us a look at the harvest at the end of time. There is no doubt that the person seated on the cloud is Jesus, who is making His return to earth. Jesus is coming this time not as a baby in a manger, but as the triumphant Lord with the power of reaping the earth. Make no mistake about it; the Lord is in charge and this age will end just how and when He desires it to end. There is no power anywhere that can change that and we can rest assured that the timing will be perfect.

Harvest Time

Then another angel came out of the temple and called in a loud voice to him who was sitting on the cloud, "Take your sickle and reap, because the time to reap has come, for the harvest of the earth is ripe." So he who was seated on the cloud swung his sickle over the earth, and the earth was harvested. (14:15-16)

An angel appears from the heavenly temple and tells Jesus that the time of harvesting has now come and He is the person who has earned the honor of reaping. Jesus then swings His sickle and the first part of the harvest, the servants of the Most High, is reaped. This is the harvest of the wheat that Jesus had spoken about in Matthew 13:29-30. The harvest of the tares is to come.

This is the culmination of the hopes of all the ages for the saints of God. We may differ on how the Lord is coming again or even when He is coming, but Christians around the world look forward to His coming and the day of the final harvest. To predict any more than what the scripture offers would be presumptuous, but we who are in Christ believe that there will be a climax to history and it will in some way resemble what John is describing here.

Our highest goal should be to make sure that we are ready for this harvest and to help as many others get ready also. Since we don't know the timetable for this event to happen we need to be ever vigilant and working in the service of the King. We have been warned repeatedly throughout scripture that this day is coming and hopefully it will be the most glorious day of our lives. Eternity is about to begin!

The question that needs to be asked is, "Are you ready for eternity to begin?" Once we have made certain that our future rests in the grace of our Lord we can face anything, including Christ when He comes.

Judgment is Coming

Another angel came out of the temple in heaven, and he too had a sharp sickle. Still another angel, who had charge of the fire, came from the altar and called in a loud voice to him who had the sharp sickle, "Take your sharp sickle and gather the clusters of grapes from the earth's vine, because its grapes are ripe." The angel swung his sickle on the earth, gathered its grapes and threw them into the great winepress of God's wrath. They were trampled in the winepress outside the city, and blood flowed out of the press, rising as high as the horses' bridles for a distance of 1,600 stadia. (14:17-20)

Two more angels come on the scene and bring about the final judgment of God. The first angel has a sickle like that of Jesus and he is instructed by the second angel to begin the process of harvesting the tares. The metaphor of grapes and the great winepress of God are used to describe the awful fate that awaits the ungodly. As the wicked are trampled in the winepress of God's wrath, like grapes under pressure, they are completely destroyed. The point is that judgment will be universal. No one will escape. The whole picture, including the depth of the blood, is given to us in symbolic form so that we can begin to see the awfulness of the penalty when God finally crushes sin and brings all evildoers to their long awaited destiny. All of this is in parable form and perfectly coincides with what Jesus said would happen in Matthew 13:39-43.

Like the three previous visions, we come to the conclusion of mankind and the end of the story of time. John has used current events and figures from his own time, under the inspiration of the Holy Spirit, to bring us to grips with the truth of the ages. In the fourth vision John has taken us from the birth of Christ through His second coming and the ensuing events at the end of the age. The story is repeated for emphasis because the matter has been decided. This old world is coming to an end and all who have lived will receive judgment on their lives.

The Fifth Vision: Revelation 15:1–19:10

We are now again taken through the whole range of God's judgments. This vision, like previous visions, covers all of the Christian era and brings us down to the end of time. In the fifteenth chapter there is a picture of the continuous praise party in the presence of God once again and there is also the announcing of the bowls, or plagues, or God's wrath from the heavenly tabernacle. In chapter sixteen these bowls of judgment are poured out on mankind that throughout history has refused to honor God. These bowls are another way of representing God's judgment—just like the seals and the trumpets. (15:1–19:10)

1. **The first bowl** – Painful sores are on the people who have the mark of the beast. This tells us that Christians are not the recipients of this judgment. People get what they have earned. (16:2)
2. **The second bowl** – The sea produces death. This, like others, is an image from the plagues on Egypt from the Old Testament. (16:3)
3. **The third bowl** – Judgment falls upon the fresh water, but here "the waters" takes on the personality of living beings. The waters symbolize a wicked government that has caused Christians to be martyred. (16:4-7)
4. **The fourth bowl** – Like the fourth trumpet, places a curse on the sun. Instead of a source of warmth, it burns people in judgment. It doesn't make people repent however, for they curse God all the more. (16:8-9)
5. **The fifth bowl** – Judgment falls directly on godless governments and the result is darkness. They become incapable of finding light. Whenever people refuse to walk in the light, they

will remain in darkness and curse God for their blindness. (16:10-11)
6. **The sixth bowl** – Physical protection (the Euphrates River) is taken away and the wicked nation is now vulnerable to invasion. Throughout history, whenever any nation becomes spiritually dead, God always allows some other nation or nations to destroy her and take her place of prominence. This is true for individuals as well. Armageddon happens whenever the battle for right versus wrong has its final conflict. Every believer has faced Armageddon, for that is where Jesus becomes Lord. (16:12-16)
7. **The seventh bowl** – Judgment is now declared to be complete and the curtain of history comes down. All will face the One on the throne and receive either justice or mercy. (16:17-21)

Chapters 17-18 are an inset of what has happened in chapters 15-16. They tell in detail the judgments that fall on an unbelieving world. There is a brief interlude, followed by a graphic description of the great prostitute (source of evil—for John, this is Rome) and the beast (tools of evil—emperors) upon which she sits. Judgment falls upon the wicked power, referred to in chapter eighteen as Babylon. Those who have profited from her: the kings of the earth, the merchants who did business with her, and the shipmasters, are all amazed at the totality of her destruction and mourn her loss. At the end of time, all evil empires meet their end and their destruction will be complete under the judgment of God.

Chapter nineteen takes us back to the praise party, or victory celebration that goes on continually around the throne of God and climaxes at the end of the age. Heaven is not a place of idleness, but a continual cathedral of praise.

A Wake Up Call

I saw in heaven another great and marvelous sign: seven angels with the seven last plagues–last, because with them God's wrath is completed. (15:1)

This chapter, as much as any other, shows how John causes Revelation to be saturated with Old Testament scriptures. We are given here another view of the praise party of chapters four and seven. The point of the passage is simple. God is the Almighty and is worthy of our praise not only because of His character, but also because of His tremendous works.

We are also again taken through the whole range of God's judgments. This vision, like the previous visions, covers all of the Christian era and brings us down to the end. This is a good example of the fact that Revelation is not written in chronological order. In each of the previous accounts we were told of some things that will not happen until the end of time and of some things that are in the realm of human history. We are going to now see some of the same process again, but now with a greater stress on the finality of God's work. The coming judgments refer to the end, but we are reminded that in our time as well that rebellion against God will bring about catastrophic penalties.

John begins the new vision by introducing another tremendous sign. Seven angels with seven plagues are about to be unleashed. These are the efforts of God to get the attention of a sinful world.

How great is the love of God that He should go to such lengths to get our attention. We see here that God cares so much about His creation that He will even bring judgments against the world in order to send a wake up call.

The Joy of Victory

And I saw what looked like a sea of glass mixed with fire and, standing beside the sea, those who had been victorious over the beast and his image and over the number of his name. They held harps given them by God... (15:2)

The scene is in heaven and we are again taken to the shores of the crystal sea, which we had viewed in 4:6. We see fire mixed with the sea, referring in symbolism to the judgment of God, as the scriptures often do (Exodus 9:24; Matthew 3:12; Hebrews 12:29). The scene is meant to bring the judgment of God into clear focus. There is perhaps some symbolism from Exodus here as a heavenly Red Sea. The martyrs had already crossed over into the Promised Land and now this sea was about to engulf their enemies.

Along with this image of a place, John sees an image of a people. It is a victorious people. In the early church, the day of a man's martyrdom was often called the day of his victory. These saints had been victorious over all that the world and Satan could throw at them. They are the redeemed, sealed by the blood of the Lamb, instead of being marked with a heart of sin from the evil one. They hold harps and join in a song of triumph! Unlike previous visions, in this vision of the bowls the message of comfort comes at the beginning—before the hand of God in judgment falls.

We are not victims of the antics of this world. We are victors! We need not fear the outcome for it has already been decided. The redeemed of the Lord triumph! We may not seem to be living triumphal existences because we often see only the small picture. God wants us to see the big view with eyes of faith. That is where we get our strength, for in faith we see what really is.

Practicing For Forever

They held the harps given them by God and sang the song of Moses the servant of God and the song of the Lamb: "Great and marvelous are your deeds, Lord God Almighty. Just and true are your ways, King of the ages. Who will not fear you, O Lord, and bring glory to your name? For you alone are holy. All nations will come and worship before you, for your righteous acts have been revealed." (15:3-4)

This heavenly victory song is made up almost entirely of Old Testament references (Psalm 86:9; 111:2; 145:17; Isaiah 66:23; Jeremiah 10:7). The singers are those who have overcome the sea of persecution just as in the story of the Exodus from Egypt the Israelites overcame the barrier of the Red Sea to make their escape. Throughout Jewish history the Israelites sang the song of Moses at the time of the evening sacrifice and here in the heavenly realms the redeemed sing it again, only with a new meaning. Here it is a celebration of an even greater redemption. The song of the Lamb is a song of praise. It is a song that all who have overcome through His name can sing. All who sing know that it is not through his or her achievements that they can join in on the celebration, but through the mercy of Christ! It is a song of praise to Him.

People who don't enjoy times of praise in local worship services will probably not be very comfortable in the heavenly realms for where God abides is always the scene of highest praise. That's why we should be practicing for eternity by lifting our voices in praise to God on a daily basis. Even if we can't sing well the Apostle Paul urges us to "Sing and make music in your hearts to the Lord, always giving thanks to God the Father for everything, in the name of our Lord Jesus Christ" (Ephesians 5:19-20). We may have a voice like an old crow, but He deserves the praise and we need the practice.

Falling Down to Look Up

After this I looked and in heaven the temple, that is, the tabernacle of the Testimony, was opened. Out of the temple came the seven angels with the seven plagues. They were dressed in clean, shining linen and wore golden sashes around their chests. Then one of the four living creatures gave to the seven angels seven golden bowls filled with the wrath of God, who lives for ever and ever. (15:5-7)

Again we find John thinking back to his Old Testament roots as he describes the opening of the "tabernacle of the Testimony," or the "Tent of Witness." No doubt he is referring to the tabernacle used by the Israelites on their trek to Canaan since he has mentioned the Song of Moses. This explanation would seem more likely than the verse being a reference to the temple in Jerusalem, which was destroyed in A.D. 70.

Seven angels come out of the presence of God. They are angels who are splendid in their dress, but fearsome in their purpose. These angels have the seven plagues of the wrath of God. One of the four living creatures (which represent all creation) gives the angels their assignment. It is a picture of the laws and forces of nature giving into the hands of the angels the plagues of a broken world. Someone has said that this is the toll that nature collects from her disobedient children. Much like what we have already witnessed in chapter eight, these bowls of wrath are to bring disaster in nature to the world.

It is never easy to understand why bad things have to happen. It certainly is not because God is cruel and vindictive. Judgments of God knock us down so that we will look up and recognize Him and draw closer to Him. Every trial that comes into the way of a lost lamb is meant to point him or her to the source of ultimate safety.

God is God

And the temple was filled with smoke from the glory of God and from his power, and no one could enter the temple until the seven plagues of the seven angels were completed. (15:8)

This is the verse of terror. It is filled with suspense and anticipation. It is the time of the final judgment of God as the bowls are about to be poured out. The fate of mankind has been sealed, for no one can enter the presence of the Lord to intercede for them. The night of doom has fallen and no prayer can stop the judgment that is coming. The image that comes to us here is much like that of Isaiah 6:4. Smoke rolls and angels fly as God moves into the lives of men. This also brings to mind the account of Moses in Exodus 40:34-35, where the presence of the Lord filled the tabernacle and Moses and the priests could not stand to minister because of the glory of the Lord. The stage is now set for chapter sixteen and the pouring out of the seven bowls of God's wrath – and Armageddon!

The writer to the Hebrews reminds us, "For we know him who said, 'It is mine to avenge; I will repay,' and again, 'The Lord will judge his people.' It is a dreadful thing to fall into the hands of the living God" (Hebrews 10:30-31). Though God has endless amounts of love and patience, He is not to be toyed with. He will continually send His message of repentance to this world in whatever way will get people's attention. There will always be many who will scoff and many who will ignore the warnings that He provides, but there will also be many who will take these warnings for what they are and repent. That is the purpose of the plagues. Even the judgments of God spring from His love for us.

The Voice of the Almighty

Then I heard a loud voice from the temple saying to the seven angels, "Go, pour out the seven bowls of God's wrath on the earth." (16:1)

Here we see the seven angels from chapter fifteen come into action. They will be pouring out plagues on mankind with their bowls. These plagues are very much like the events that took place at the blowing of the seven trumpets (chapters 8-11), but there is a difference. The trumpets only affect a third, or a portion of the earth, but these judgments are final and complete. The judgments brought about by the sounding of the trumpets did not affect men until the fifth trumpet. The pouring out of the bowls of God's wrath has an immediate effect. Destruction is complete upon the enemies of God. This fifth vision ushers in a final, terrible, and graphic picture of disaster that God hurls upon the unbelieving world. God is overthrowing all that is evil.

Previous commands had come from various characters of the heavenly realm, but this command comes from the temple itself. God Himself takes a very active part in the unfolding of this drama. The command is clear. God's wrath is to be poured out on the earth. We know it is His voice because we have just been told in 15:8 that no one else could enter the temple because of His glory. These bowls remind us of the account of the Lord's righteous wrath in Jeremiah 25:15: "This is what the Lord, the God of Israel said to me: 'Take from my hand this cup filled with the wine of my wrath and make all the nations to whom I send you drink it.'" This shows the penalty God places upon the world.

The world is not just ambling along through time. It is headed for a destination.

When God Gives Us What We Want

The first angel went and poured out his bowl on the land, and ugly and painful sores broke out on the people who had the mark of the beast and worshiped his image. (16:2)

The first plague is one of sores on the people of the land and brings to mind the sixth plague of Egypt as recorded in Exodus 9:8-12. These sores are not on the righteous, but upon the wicked who have the mark of the beast upon them and have lived accordingly. How true it is that there are some who will pay a price for the evil they have done; a price that Christians will never have to pay.

We must be careful not to see God as a human here. He is not finally fed up with sinners in the world and lashes out at them in anger. He is simple fulfilling the sowing and reaping laws that He established long ago. As sinners choose sin, they will reap the punishment of sin. God is not behaving in a fitful rage for He is simply being just. The situation is exactly the same in Romans 1:18-32. God lets mankind reap the rewards of the lifestyle they have chosen to follow.

God is like that. He gives us what we want. If we choose to follow Him and His directions for our lives then we will gain the benefits that come from such a relationship. If we choose to ignore Him and put Him out of our thoughts then we will reap the emptiness and pain that result from such a choice. It's the same way with our children. We can invite them to obey the rules of the house and the result will be harmony. If they choose to break them and go their own way they will bring the consequences that come with that choice upon each person. We can teach people not to touch the hot stove, but if they ignore our warnings then they will be burned no matter how much we wish it wasn't so.

There is No Place to Hide

The second angel poured out his bowl on the sea, and it turned into blood like that of a dead man, and every living thing in the sea died. (16:3)

As the second angel empties his bowl on the sea, John sees the plague as coagulated blood. It is deadly to all creatures touched by it. Again we see the images that John pulls from the Old Testament plagues in Egypt. The first plague recorded was a plague of blood "over the waters of Egypt—over the streams and canals, over the ponds and reservoirs—and they will turn to blood" (Exodus 7:19). In the original catastrophe all the fish died and the smell became so foul that people couldn't drink the water.

The idea behind this bowl of plague signifies completeness. None who are guilty will escape the wrath of God. Even though men and women have hidden their sins from the prying eyes of society, our Father in heaven knows not only the actions committed in secret, but also the very thoughts and desires that motivated those actions.

Perhaps the Psalmist said it best: "Where can I go from your Spirit? Where can I flee from your presence? If I go up to the heavens, you are there; if I make my bed in the depths, you are there" (Psalm 139: 7-8). Just as the righteous are never out of the Lord's care, the unrighteous are never out of His all-discerning view and as the Apostle Paul said to the Romans: "Because of your stubbornness and your unrepentant heart, you are storing up wrath again yourself for the day of God's wrath, when his righteous judgment will be revealed. God will give to each person according to what he has done" (Romans 2:5-6).

It is never pleasant to think about judgment, but it is prudent.

Fair is Fair

The third angel poured out his bowl on the rivers and springs of water, and they became blood. Then I heard the angel in charge of the waters say: "You are just in these judgments, you who are and who were, the Holy One, because you have so judged; for they have shed the blood of your saints and prophets, and you have given them blood to drink as they deserve." And I heard the altar respond: "Yes, Lord God Almighty, true and just are your judgments." (16:4-7)

As happened with the blowing of the trumpets, first the seas, then the fresh water is to feel the effects of judgment. The waters in both these plagues are personified as participants in a wicked government, which had caused the righteous to become martyrs. The angel in charge of the waters bears witness that God's judgment is fair because they (these waters) have spilled the blood of the righteous. Now they too will reap what they have sown (Galatians 6:7). Water in itself cannot be a culprit. The waters represent the evil ones in charge who have done such things to God's people.

The voice (most likely meaning the saints under the altar: 6:9; 8:3) echoes the sentiments of the angel. God is not out of control. He is just and fair in giving the wicked what they have earned.

I have known pastors and biblical scholars who dismiss the wrath of God as being out of character for the divine. They quote verses saying, "God is love" (I John 4:8) or every Christian's favorite, John 3:16. However, what many fail to realize is that there can be no love without discipline and correction. There must be penalties in order for there to be justice. If God just turned His head and gave everyone a free pass to eternal life regardless of how they lived or where their loyalties lie, where would the justice be? No, God is going to balance the scales and if we suffer His wrath, it will be because of our choice, not His.

When Hearts Get Hard...

The fourth angel poured out his bowl on the sun, and the sun was given power to scorch people with fire. They were seared by the intense heat and they cursed the name of God, who had control over these plagues, but they refused to repent and glorify him. (16:8-9)

When the fourth bowl is poured out, like its counterpart—the fourth trumpet—it affects the sun and changes what should be a blessing of warmth into a curse. Instead of darkness as earlier seen, now the curse is in the form of intense heat. Though men are scorched by the sun's heat, they do not recognize God's hand at work. In fact, instead of repenting for their sins, they curse God for their sufferings. John notes that God is the one who is responsible for the plague. He is sovereign and is in control of the whole process of mankind to the end.

It should become clear by now that John is repeating himself and telling the same story that he has told earlier. Each vision is telling the story of the history of the Church age from its beginning right down to the end of time. The seals, the trumpets, and the bowls of wrath are different views of the same events. John, inspired by the Holy Spirit, uses this unique style of writing to confuse those who would do the Church and him harm, but in such a way that believers of his day would easily recognize the symbolism offered.

How sad it is that men often do not learn from their suffering, but only get harder. Perhaps our prayer should be not so much that God would change lives, but that He would allow the disciplines He sends to soften the hearts of the recipients. Simeon prophesied that Jesus would be responsible for the falling and rising of men (Luke2:34). Unless a person is brought down they will never look up to God. Pray that men and women may fall so that they may rise.

Boxing with God

The fifth angel poured out his bowl on the throne of the beast, and his kingdom was plunged into darkness. Men gnawed their tongues in agony and cursed the God of heaven because of their pains and their sores, but they refused to repent of what they had done. (16:10-11)

Now God's wrath falls directly on the center of the beast's government instead of just on his subjects. The darkness of sin is taking its toll and we begin to see the plagues passing from the physical into the spiritual realm. The effects of all the earlier plagues are still upon the sinners of the world and they "gnaw their tongues in pain." The kingdom of the beast always takes a terrible toll on those who side with it. All over the world today there are people who are directly suffering from the ravages of being "on Satan's side" and are lost in a realm of spiritual darkness. But as before, people in the darkness of sin do not readily reach for "the Light." Instead, they curse God for the suffering even it is Satan who has brought about their pain. They do not seek forgiveness. Pain does not draw men to God—only the Holy Spirit does. They who are suffering are like Pharaoh, who hardened his heart to God's call.

There will always be kings and kingdoms that think they are invincible. They rattle their swords and shake their fists at the rest of the world and in the face of God Himself without a thought that what they offer is just false bravado. Any student of history can tell us that for as long as there have been people there have been kingdoms rising and falling. None are as powerful as they think they are.

When the day of final day judgment comes upon the nations of this world they will realize all too late that they are only as strong as their faith in the Living God.

Judgment Through the Hands of Others

The sixth angel poured out his bowl on the great river Euphrates, and its water was dried up to prepare the way for the kings from the East. (16:12)

Many times in the Old Testament the drying up of water was a sign of the power of God (Exodus 14:21; Joshua 3:17; Isaiah 11:16; Jeremiah 51:36; Zechariah 10:11). As the sixth bowl is poured out, it falls directly on the Euphrates River and results in its drying up. This river has always been seen as a literal and symbolic protection against enemies who would try to cross over and conquer. The barrier of protection is now removed and war is imminent.

In the Hebrew mind, Israel's enemies always came out of the east. This is because of their background of bondage to the Assyrians and Babylonians. In John's day the great threat from the east for the Roman Empire was an invasion from the Parthians, who lived in the area just south of the Caspian Sea. This group provided some of the strongest resistance to the expanding of the Roman Empire. This is John's way of showing the judgment of God falling on the wicked empire, but it could also refer to any nation however, even us. Throughout history, whenever any nation has become rotten at the core of its being and becomes spiritually dead, God always allows some other nation or nations to destroy her and take her place of prominence.

This is where we see the "both/and" of this book. It is written not only to describe the final judgments of God, but also the current judgments of God. It is meant to inspire Christians of all ages that the unrighteous rulers and kingdoms will not always have their own way. In this life, and certainly at the end of the age, God always has a way of evening the score. We can count on it!

Our Response to Conflict

Then I saw three evil spirits that looked like frogs; they came out of the mouth of the dragon, out of the mouth of the beast and out of the mouth of the false prophet. They are spirits of demons performing miraculous signs, and they go out to the kings of the whole world, to gather them for the battle on the great day of God Almighty. (16:13-14)

Here we see the demonic powers at work against God's true righteousness. The "great day of God Almighty" is a graphic way of describing the deciding day of conflict between the worship of the power of the earth (which for John is the Roman Empire) and the worship of God. The demons are deceiving the kings of the world as they lead them to side against the King of all kings.

Kingdoms don't go astray on their own. John is bringing out the point that there is organized evil at work when leaders of nations rebel against God. Evil has a source and it is the enemy of our souls. The Apostle Peter reminds us: "Be self-controlled and alert. Your enemy the devil prowls around like a roaring lion looking for someone to devour" (I Peter 5:8). Just as Satan is out to destroy our souls, he often works through the leaders of nations to do his dirty work. His demons incite the riots, bloodshed, and violence that have become so much a part of our daily news in many parts of the world.

What should our response be to all this? We should look at these conflicts as the Apostle Paul did: "All this is from God, who reconciled us to himself through Christ and gave us the ministry of reconciliation: that God was reconciling the world to himself in Christ, not counting men's sins against them. And he has committed to us the message of reconciliation. We are therefore Christ's ambassadors, as though God were making his appeal through us. We implore you on Christ's behalf: Be reconciled to God" (II Corinthians 5:18-20).

Being Holy

"Behold, I come like a thief! Blessed is he who stays awake and keeps his clothes with him, so that he may not go naked and be shamefully exposed." (16:15)

This is another short interlude of warning to the Church. It is versed in much the same language as the Apostle Paul uses in I Thessalonians 5:2, "for you know very well that the day of the Lord will come like a thief in the night." In the midst of all the pain and suffering that goes on in the world as a result of mankind running after sinful activities, the Church is admonished to be faithful and alert. There is constantly the danger that the saints will give up on their walk with Christ because of the pressures of the world. The Holy Spirit inspires John to add these words of warning. We are to always be ready because no one knows when the Lord will return for His Church and bring time to an end.

Holiness is not just a crisis at a place of prayer. It is a relationship that one has with the Lord God. As in any relationship there are times of ebb and flow. We would like to think that we will always have a feeling of closeness and intimacy with Jesus, but our emotions can fool us. Though the grace of God never changes and the power to hold us is strong enough to weather any storm, we in our weakness sometimes have a tendency to let go of His almighty hand.

It is in this relationship that John offers his warning. At the time of this writing he has been around Christians long enough to know how fickle they can sometimes be. He warns us to always be on guard against the enemy of our souls and to be ready in our walk with the Master. Though God is not willing that any should be lost—especially those who have started the good walk with Him—we must stay awake and hold fast to the grace that has been offered to us.

Armageddon Now

Then they gathered the kings together to the place that in Hebrew is called Armageddon. (16:16)

The dragon is hard at work in this scene because he has not only engaged the beast (most likely—Rome), and the false prophet (the second beast of 13:11—organized religion), but also the governments of the rest of the world. A great battle between the forces of good and the forces of evil is set to begin at a place called Armageddon.

Without doubt, the idea comes from Jewish history for this place, translated as the Plain of Megiddo, where many battles of the Hebrew people had been fought. Some see this as a time when all the nations of the world will gather to do battle with the united people of God. The outcomes of the battle would prove to be the victor forever.

Another view however, and one that stays in context with the scope of this study, sees this as a different kind of battle than one of actual blood and physical warfare. The battle of Armageddon is a symbolic battle. It has no geographic location or specific point in time. The final battle of good verses evil takes place in the heart of every individual. It is a spiritual decision, not a physical battle. Some people are in the midst of their Armageddon right now, for they are struggling over who will have control of their soul and their life for eternity. It is the place and time when a person says a final "Yes" to the one who will be their master. Armageddon is not an event that happens as Christ is returning for His own at the end of time. It is an event that takes place whenever the great final spiritual struggle for a person's soul is taking place.

The Final Bowl

The seventh angel poured out his bowl into the air, and out of the temple came a loud voice from the throne, saying, "It is done!" Then there came flashes of lightning, rumblings, peals of thunder and a severe earthquake. No earthquake like it has ever occurred since man has been on earth, so tremendous was the quake. The great city split into three parts, and the cities of the nations collapsed. God remembered Babylon the Great and gave her the cup filled with the wine of the fury of his wrath. Every island fled away and the mountains could not be found. From the sky huge hailstones of about a hundred pounds each fell upon men. And they cursed God on account of the plague of hail, because the plague was so terrible. (16:17-21)

As the last of the seven angels pours out his bowl of wrath, the voice of the Lord declares that the judgment and time have now been completed. We have come to this point in other parts of this book (8:5, 11:19, 14:16). This is the end of the plague and time will be no more. All that is left is the description and explanation of what has already taken place, which is justice for the wicked and mercy for the saints. As the Almighty declares the end, there is a chorus of energy in dramatic fashion. The symbolism is of an earthquake that rips apart the tool that has been in the dragon's hand (for John, this is the Empire of Rome—also known as Babylon the Great). The style of writing is very graphic and of course, apocalyptic in form, but the message comes across. God is in charge! Once again we see His majesty. Once again the Church is reminded that there is coming a day of justice when the powers of evil will be remembered for what they truly are. The end is coming for the world and rewards and punishments are waiting for its inhabitants. It is amazing to note that even when the curtain of mankind is falling, the wicked do not glorify God, but instead, curse Him. To make up for the wicked being unwilling to give God His due, we should never be without praise on our lips. Our Lord is worthy of all praise!

Balancing the Scales

One of the seven angels who had the seven bowls came and said to me, "Come, I will show you the punishment of the great prostitute, who sits on many waters. With her the kings of the earth committed adultery and the inhabitants of the earth were intoxicated with the wine of her adulteries." (17:1-2)

We have come to the end of the dramatic scene of the angels with the bowls of God's wrath. We have seen this drama unfold three times as the story is told about the judgment of God on an unbelieving world. First, it came in the form of seven seals and their opening brought forth judgment. Secondly, we saw it as seven trumpets ushered in terrors for an unbelieving population of the earth. Next, this picture of the seven bowls repeats the story once again. Judgment was promised and now it has come. In between each story of terror there is a message of comfort to the Church. God is truly in control. He has let the wheat and the tares grow together, but He has the last word and brings about a harvest of both the good and the evil.

We now see another interlude. It is a break between the last of the plagues of God and the final scene of reward and punishment. We find these next chapters as somewhat of an inset of what has happened earlier. They tell in detail about what has just happened concerning the judgments of God. The story is explained in further detail as we see the fall of Babylon (most likely as Rome by John) and the beast (the evil ally of sin). We were told in 14:8 and in 16:19 that Babylon was going to be destroyed, but now we see how it happens. The kings of the earth, who will in turn be judged by God, will destroy it. We are headed toward the great and terrible, final confrontation with the Almighty. God will balance the scales ultimately.

The Great Prostitute

Then the angel carried me away in the Spirit into a desert. There I saw a woman sitting on a scarlet beast that was covered with blasphemous names and had seven heads and ten horns. The woman was dressed in purple and scarlet, and was glittering with gold, precious stones and pearls. She held a golden cup in her hand, filled with abominable things and the filth of her adulteries. (17:3-4)

In 4:2 we saw that John was "in the Spirit," and we have also already seen the phrase "into the desert," in 12:6, and 14, when John was trying to relate the difference between the Church and the world that is not in Christ. The "desert" signifies a place that is away from the threat of the world and is safe in the presence of God. Though protected from the wrath of God, the Church (in this instance, John) can view the events that take place on a sinful world. Then, as well as now, the Church needs to spend more time "in the desert" so that it can receive the message that God wants to give.

John sees a woman, or prostitute. The prophet Nahum spoke of Nineveh as a prostitute (3:4), Isaiah calls Tyre by the same name in 23:16-17, and the idea of prostitution or harlotry is a symbol for religious apostasy through the book of Hosea. The scarlet woman is the pagan city of Rome. She is dressed in royal garb and holds in her hand all the evils and terrible things associated with her existence.

We also see that the woman is sitting upon a scarlet beast and upon many waters. The beast is identified in 13:1, 3, 14, and 19:20. It is the political power of Rome, but one must also be quick to note that this is what John sees for his time. It can be equated with any power of any time that yields itself to Satan and spreads its influence like historical Rome.

Avoiding the Great Sin

This title was written on her forehead: MYSTERY BABYLON THE GREAT THE MOTHER OF PROSTITUTES AND OF THE ABOMINATIONS OF THE EARTH. (17:5)

It is said that the woman has names written on her forehead. The word "mystery" is used, but mystery does not mean in Greek thought what we normally associate with it in American culture. Something may be mysterious to the onlooker, but not at all mysterious to one who is on the inside workings. We could find that this truth has many parallels in our own society. The mystery here is that Babylon is actually Rome and Rome is the center of all of the evil that is plaguing the Church of John's day.

We also see that the woman is sitting upon a scarlet beast and upon many waters. As waters flow out of a central source to many world areas, so goes the influence of the evil Roman Empire.

The United States has been called "the Great Satan" by many in the Islamic world. Though the accuracy of that charge may be questioned, the imagery and symbolism is the same as we see here. So, the lesson should be clear for us. Any nation that leaves its trust in the one true God and sells its soul for commerce, power, and influence becomes a "beast" and "prostitutes" itself on the stages of the world.

May God help us to look beyond national loyalty, whatever country we come from and look to the unity that is found in Christ! To avoid being part of the "Babylon" John writes about we need to focus on being a part of "the church of the firstborn, whose names are written in heaven" (Hebrews 12:23). What is below will pass; what is above is eternal.

The Price of Blood

I saw that the woman was drunk with the blood of the saints, the blood of those who bore testimony to Jesus. When I saw her, I was greatly astonished. (17:6)

The scarlet color of the woman is due to the blood of the saints that she has spilled. This verse is a testimony to the saints who have suffered, but is also incriminating evidence to the murderer in question. She is so appalling that John is amazed, much as were the allies of World War II when they liberated the Nazi death camps.

There is so much blood shed in the world on a daily basis. We like to think that we as civilized people have moved beyond this terrible tragedy, but all one has to do to realize that this is not so is to watch the evening news for a half-hour. Whether in the continent of Africa, the streets of North America, the sweatshops in Indonesia or China, or war-torn battlefields, bloodshed is still a reality of life.

What John sees here however is the prostitute who is drunk with the blood of the saints. Here again we like to think we have moved beyond that time, but we have to admit that it is so. The gospel is continuing to spread around the world, but often not without great sacrifice—often of life and limb. Christians are still "hard pressed on every side, but not crushed; persecuted, but not abandoned; struck down, but not destroyed" (II Corinthians 4:8-9). Many are paying a great price to simply be able to share the words of life. John lets us know that such sacrifice has not gone unnoticed. Even those who are killed die only for a moment and then life eternal is theirs.

The Mystery Explained

Then the angel said to me: "Why are you astonished? I will explain to you the mystery of the woman and of the beast she rides, which has the seven heads and ten horns. The beast, which you saw, once was, now is not, and will come up out of the Abyss and go to his destruction. The inhabitants of the earth whose names have not been written in the book of life from the creation of the world will be astonished when hey see the beast, because he once was, now is not, and yet will come. "This calls for a mind with wisdom. The seven heads are seven hills on which the woman sits. They are also seven kings. Five have fallen, one is, the other has not yet come; but when he does come, he must remain for a little while. The beast who once was, and now is not, is an eighth king. He belongs to the seven and is going to his destruction. (17:7-11)

An explanation is now in order for John because what he is seeing is more than he can comprehend. The angel explains that the beast is the anti-Christ empire of Rome and that he will be destroyed. The seven heads are the seven hills of Rome and also said to be seven kings (vs.10). Perhaps this is another way of seeing the progression of the evil empire through which the people of God had come at John's time. Some have noted that Egypt, Assyria, Babylon, Persian, and Greece had all fallen by this time. Rome would be the sixth, and a seventh one was still to come—possibly the Catholic Church of the Dark Ages. This is all speculation, however. The meaning of the seven heads and ten horns is symbolic and tells us that any nation or power that raises itself up against God will eventually go down to destruction.

The beast mentioned is most likely seen by John to be Nero. Nero was one of the most wicked kings, but when he died he was replaced by Domitian, who seemed to surpass even Nero in cruelty. It was not the man that was reborn, but the terrible injustices that the empire heaped upon Christianity. Certainly the spirit of Nero lived again.

What Goes Around, Comes Around

"The ten horns you saw are ten kings who have not yet received a kingdom, but who for one hour will receive authority as kings along with the beast. They have one purpose and will give their power and authority to the beast. They will make war against the Lamb, but the Lamb will overcome them because he is Lord of lords and King of kings—and with him will be his called, chosen and faithful followers." Then the angel said to me, "The waters you saw, where the prostitute sits, are peoples, multitudes, nations and languages. The beast and the ten horns you saw will hate the prostitute. They will bring her to ruin and leave her naked; they will eat her flesh and burn her with fire. For God has put it into their hearts to accomplish his purpose by agreeing to give the beast their power to rule, until God's words are fulfilled. The woman you saw is the great city that rules over the kings of the earth." (17:12-18)

In these verses we see that the harlot has as her confederates the rulers of the earth. For a time they are joined together in their self-serving, greedy purpose, but it will not last. They continued to make war against the Church of Jesus Christ throughout the ages, but always are destined to fail in their attempts to destroy her. The Lamb is supreme. His cause is righteous and will never be overcome. These are great words of encouragement to all believers. Though civil authorities, society in general, and all the powers of hell stand against the faithful of Christ, the eternal kingdom and purpose of the Lamb will always be triumphant. Eventually, even allies of evil will turn on her and help bring about her destruction. God has used many instances of the powers of an evil nation to over throw another evil nation.

As God turned His wrath on a rebellious people in days gone by and brought their destruction, He can surely do it again. He is in control and is orchestrating every event, right down to the close of the drama of human history. Even those who are rebelling against Him are merely pawns in the game of life. God does not change and His power is not diminished; He reigns forever!

When Nations Leave God Out...

After this I saw another angel coming down from heaven. He had great authority, and the earth was illuminated by his splendor. With a mighty voice he shouted: "Fallen! Fallen is Babylon the Great! She has become a home for demons and a haunt for every evil spirit, a haunt for every unclean and detestable bird. For all the nations have drunk the maddening wine of her adulteries. The kings of the earth committed adultery with her, and the merchants of the earth grew rich from her excessive luxuries." (18:1-3)

As John muses over what he has witnessed in the previous chapter, namely the great prostitute who sat on the scarlet beast, he now sees another angel in the fashion of 10:1 (the third vision). Here is another clue that the message John is giving is given in a circular fashion rather than in chronological order. This angel comes down from the presence of God and still glows with the glory of being in such a heavenly environment. The language that John uses to describe the glory of God reminds us of Ezekiel 43:1. John also pulls a large number of references from Isaiah (13:19-22), Jeremiah (50:39, 51:37), Zephaniah (2:13-15), and various places in Ezekiel.

The announcement itself is one of doom for the evil city of Babylon. No doubt John sees Rome as one of the great leaders of evil in his day. The reason for her doom is also given in the announcement. She is a habitation for demons and uncleanness, and her influence has had a powerful effect on the other nations of the earth. Such was the case for Rome and for many other nations given over to evil down through the centuries.

We who live in the present need not look to the future to see this fulfilled. Doom will always come to the nation who leaves God out. It has happened throughout history and will continue to the end of time.

The Minister of Justice

Then I heard another voice from heaven say: "Come out of her, my people, so that you will not share in her sins, so that you will not receive any of her plagues; for her sins are piled up to heaven, and God has remembered her crimes. Give back to her as she has given; pay her back double for what she has done. Mix her a double portion from her own cup. Give her as much torture and grief as the glory and luxury she gave herself. In her heart she boasts, 'I sit as queen; I am not a widow, and I will never mourn.' Therefore in one day her plagues will overtake her: death, mourning and famine. She will be consumed by fire, for mighty is the Lord God who judges her. (18:4-8)

God is speaking to His people with words of warning. If the Church had already been taken out, to whom is He speaking? But even if this is not the voice of God, it is certainly one of His messengers and we must conclude that our heavenly Father is reaching out to His Church once again and warns them against the danger of even being a part of such things as go on in Babylon (Rome). The Christian is urged to separate himself from every connection with the way of evil. Of course, it is not meant that we are to leave the world, or even run off to a monastery to hide ourselves away. The idea is that the Church should keep itself clean in the midst of the grime of sin around it, but it can only do so through the power of the blood of the Lamb. As Jesus declared to His disciples, the Church is to be in the world, but not of the world (John 17:11-14). Just as we saw the woman flee into the desert in 12:14, once again the Church must flee the very appearance of evil.

This section of scripture also brings to mind the idea of punishment. Vengeance belongs to the Lord and He alone will have the responsibility of administering justice. The world may scoff and be proud in this age, but the One who is holiness personified will one day put them to shame and judgment.

Misery Loves Company

"When the kings of the earth who committed adultery with her and shared her luxury see the smoke of her burning, they will weep and mourn over her. Terrified at her torment, they will stand far off and cry: "Woe! Woe, O great city, O Babylon, city of power! In one hour your doom has come!' (18:9-10)

Here we have a dirge for the fallen city of Babylon (Rome), which is sung by the kings who are going down the drain with her. Certainly they are appalled by the measure of destruction that is falling upon the wicked. The actions and judgments as recorded by John should serve as a warning to our own nation and others around us.

Certainly John was inspired by the Holy Spirit in this writing, for Babylon (Rome) had not fallen in his time and did not fall for three and a half more centuries. He is not wishing idly that this would happen however, for it was a pronouncement of fact that was awaiting Rome and any other city, country, or institution that would rebel against the Most High. John speaks of doom as if it had already happened. With eyes of faith he sees the end. The wages of sin may seem like fun and riches for a while, but the final payday always rolls around and those without Christ will receive their true earnings of death and destruction. Even the Church is not exempt from these facts. In the fourteen and fifteen centuries it became more concerned with power and gold than with souls and became evil in its existence. Babylon is Rome, but it is more than Rome. It is anything, anyone, and anywhere that evil takes priority over good.

At the time of John's writing the empire was strong and seemingly invincible, but with eyes of faith he sees what waits for this great evil lady. She has made her bed with the devil and she is going to have to lie in it.

Falling Hard

"The merchants of the earth will weep and mourn over her because no one buys their cargoes any more—cargoes of gold, silver, precious stones and pearls; fine linen, purple, silk and scarlet cloth; every sort of citron wood, and articles of every kind made of ivory, costly wood, bronze, iron and marble; cargoes of cinnamon and spice, of incense, myrrh and frankincense, of wine and olive oil, of fine flour and wheat; cattle and sheep; horses and carriages; and bodies and souls of men. "They will say, 'The fruit you longed for is gone from you. All your riches and splendor have vanished, never to be recovered.' The merchants who sold these things and gained their wealth from her will stand far off, terrified at her torment. They will weep and mourn and cry out:" 'Woe! Woe, O great city, dressed in fine linen, purple and scarlet, and glittering with gold, precious stones and pearls! (18:11-16)

These verses are a song of doom as given by the merchants who did business with Babylon. All who side with this force of evil will share in her suffering and destruction. At the time of John's writing, the world was pouring its riches into Rome and trade for profit was the order of the day. Men have sold their souls for money and now we see just what the Lord thinks of those who put material gain above holiness. The background of this passage is Ezekiel 26-27. We see men who lament the passing of Babylon purely from a selfish point of view. They aren't sorry for the sin that is rampant. They are merely sorry that the source of their income is ending.

Chapter eighteen is a *doom-song* about the fall of the evil empire, but chapter nineteen is a hallelujah response of victory for the people of God. As John has done in other places, he tells a story of wrath for mankind followed by a chorus of comfort for the Church. We see this pattern now once again.

The wicked will be punished and the righteous will be rewarded. That is the message that comes throughout the gospel. It was true for the years gone by, it is true today, and will be true at the end of the age.

The Root of Selfishness

In one hour such great wealth has been brought to ruin!' "Every sea captain, and all who travel by ship, the sailors, and all who earn their living from the sea, will stand far off. When they see the smoke of her burning, they will exclaim, 'Was there ever a city like this great city?' They will throw dust on their heads, and with weeping and mourning cry out:" 'Woe! Woe, O great city, where all who had ships on the sea became rich through her wealth! In one hour she has been brought to ruin! (18:17-19)

This is the last of the trio of laments. First it came from the kings of the earth, then from the merchants who made their profits off Babylon (Rome), and now the dirge comes from the shipmasters. Again we see much of Ezekiel's description of the fall of Tyre (Ezekiel 27:28-30). The sad thing of these laments is the fact that they are not feeling sorry at all for the falling city; they are only sorry for themselves.

What a commentary on the state of sinful man. When all around people are suffering, the sinner can only think of himself. How different is this attitude from the Christ who gave up everything for us simply because He loves us. The lesson from this chapter is clear: The world will continue in its sinning ways until the day God's judgment falls upon it. Life without Christ is a continuing picture of selfishness and greed running headlong into destruction. The Word of God is sure however, for destruction is truly coming and on that final day the world without Christ will truly mourn.

We who are in Christ always need to set a different attitude. Instead of kicking those who are down, our job is to lift others up—even those who don't deserve such consideration. Remember, Christ died to redeem those who were not deserving of His sacrifice. Every member of mankind should be shown the same grace from Christians as from Christ.

The End Will Come

Rejoice over her, O heaven! Rejoice, saints and apostles and prophets! God has judged her for the way she treated you."' Then a mighty angel picked up a boulder the size of a large millstone and threw it into the sea, and said: "With such violence the great city of Babylon will be thrown down, never to be found again. The music of harpists and musicians, flute players and trumpeters, will never be heard in you again. No workman of any trade will ever be found in you again. The sound of a millstone will never be heard in you again. The light of a lamp will never shine in you again. The voice of bridegroom and bride will never be heard in you again. Your merchants were the world's great men. By your magic spell all the nations were led astray. In her was found the blood of prophets and of the saints, and of all who have been killed on the earth." (18:20-24)

In this final section of this chapter we see the scene change somewhat from a cry of mourning to a song of rejoicing. The characters in the story are different however. Now it is the righteous ones who are instructed to rejoice because their day of victory and retribution is at hand. It is not the picture that we think of when we remember the words of Jesus telling us to rejoice when men persecute us for His sake (Matthew 5:11-12), but it is truly the voice of faith that is speaking. No one who is on the side of evil can win and no one who is on the side of righteousness can lose ultimately. Also we see that rejoicing over the downfall of Babylon is not personal. It is God that has been sinned against and now it is God who is triumphing. Their joy is over His victory.

As we see the final picture of the destruction of Babylon (Rome), we see a large millstone being thrown into the sea, never to be seen again. This is symbolism at its finest. Just as the rock sinks beneath the waves of the sea, so also is the city of sin gone forever. Never again will the noisy sound of sin raise its ugly head. It is truly a time for the righteous to rejoice for the Lord is on His throne and an eternity of joy is upon the people of God.

The Praise Party Goes On

After this I heard what sounded like the roar of a great multitude in heaven shouting: "Hallelujah! Salvation and glory and power belong to our God, for true and just are his judgments. He has condemned the great prostitute who corrupted the earth by her adulteries. He has avenged on her the blood of his servants." And again they shouted: "Hallelujah! The smoke from her goes up for ever and ever." (19:1-3)

If the book of Revelation is anything, it is a book of extremes. Chapter eighteen that we just finished is full of doom and woe and now this chapter is completely the opposite. However, it seems very obvious that the first ten verses of chapter nineteen are linked to chapter eighteen. We see here a wonderful chorus of praise. Instead of the deathly quietness of Babylon we hear "Hallelujahs!" This passage fits well with other sections of scripture in this book where a great praise party is going on (chapters 4, 5, 7, 11, 15, and 16).

Here we see that heaven is not a quiet place of meditation and resting, but a place of joyous praise. John hears the roar of voices and immediately is reminded of a large gathering of people. The message shouted out is one of praise to the Almighty and His attributes are lauded, as well as His deeds justified. The word *"Hallelujah"* is not used in any other part of the New Testament, but it has a Hebrew counterpart in many of the Psalms.

The voices that John hears coming from the combined groups of heaven are much like what we see in 7:9-12, along with all the host of the redeemed. This song is part of the climax of this vision and we see the end arriving once again just as we have in other parts of this book of repetition. We see that God is vindicated for His actions because His deeds are fair in light of the great sins of Babylon. A righteous judgment is upon her and will continue forever.

The Wedding of the Lamb

The twenty-four elders and the four living creatures fell down and worshiped God, who was seated on the throne. And they cried: "Amen, Hallelujah!" Then a voice came from the throne, saying: "Praise our God, all you his servants, you who fear him, both small and great!" Then I heard what sounded like a great multitude, like the roar of rushing waters and like loud peals of thunder, shouting: "Hallelujah! For our Lord God Almighty reigns. Let us rejoice and be glad and give him glory! For the wedding of the Lamb has come, and his bride has made herself ready. Fine linen, bright and clean, was given her to wear." (Fine linen stands for the righteous acts of the saints.) (19:4-8)

In answer to the chorus of praise from the great multitude we see the uniting of the twenty-four elders and the four living creatures (the Church universal and all creation) with a proclamation of approval concerning the message given.

Following the note of united heavenly approval, a voice comes directly from the throne. The Godhead speaks and informs all His people as to their responsibility of praise. Once more John hears a great multitude of voices, as powerful as a waterfall and as clear as thunder. The voices are not necessarily echoing the previous chorus, though it is a tribute of praise, but here we see the redeemed of God looking ahead to the climactic wedding of the Lamb. The bride (the Church) has proven herself by the grace of God to be ready for the eternal uniting with the Son of God. She has remained pure in a dirty world and has overcome all the traps of Satan and now she is to be given in marriage to the Prince of Peace. This does not take place until chapter twenty-one, but we are given a bit of a preview here. Jesus Himself had spoken of this event in Matthew 26:29. In John's mind, the Day of the Lord was not something to be feared, but a time of great rejoicing and celebration. The righteous deeds of the people of God (fine linen) are a trophy the bride (the Church) can still give to her groom (Jesus).

The Spirit of Prophecy

Then the angel said to me, "Write: 'Blessed are those who are invited to the wedding supper of the Lamb!'" And he added, "These are the true words of God." At this I fell at his feet to worship him. But he said to me, "Do not do it! I am a fellow servant with you and with your brothers who hold to the testimony of Jesus. Worship God! For the testimony of Jesus is the spirit of prophecy." (19:9-10)

The angel mentioned here is apparently the same one that spoke to John concerning the doom of Babylon back in 18:1. The beatitude he gives is for the Church and has come from the very lips of God Himself. John is overwhelmed by this message and by what he has been witnessing. He falls before this mighty being to worship. He is rebuked however, because only God is worthy of such adoration.

It could very well be that angel worship seemed to be a problem among the churches of Asia Minor, and that John includes this message for the purpose of instruction as well as inspiration.

We see here that all created beings are to be servants of God and that He is worshipped through the Son, Jesus Christ. This validates again the Christian message that Jesus truly is the Son of God and is co-equal with Him. Certainly it is telling of the message of Jesus that brings to the world the *Good News*. Prophecy is not so much *foretelling* in the Bible as it is *forth telling*. That's a good rule of thumb for all Bible study as well as this book. All true prophecy bears witness to Jesus and that is the message of this book. It is "The Revelation of Jesus Christ!" It's all about Him. He is all that mattered when it was written and He is all that matters now.

The Sixth Vision: Revelation 19:11–20:15

We see again that the visions are not in chronological order as we now again cover the whole of history between the first and second comings of Christ. The first image we see is of Jesus as the all-conquering King. He is above all and that gives hope to the Church.

As a result of the judgment of the King, those who have been defeated in the battle of Armageddon (those who have not proclaimed Christ as Lord in their hearts and lives) are sent into eternal punishment. The feast of the birds reminds us that everyone will either be a part of the bird feast (banquet of the lost) or the marriage supper of the Lamb (banquet of the redeemed).

Satan is bound during the Church age. Those who are not destroyed and those who die in Christ are a part of the first resurrection and reign with Christ. In the end, Satan and his followers will be banished to the everlasting lake of fire as their judgment.

The Millennial Reign Views

There has probably never been a portion of scripture that has been more controversial and divisive in the Church as this one. Certainly it was never John's purpose for this part of his book to cause such schism among the people of God, so whatever interpretations and conclusions are honestly and intelligently reached here should be respected—even if they do not agree with our own views. The millennium (or 1000 years) described here, is often a basis for an entire system of eschatology (study of the end times), and that is unfortunate because the whole of scripture needs to be weighed to balance our views concerning Bible interpretation. We will deal with this problem as we go further.

There are four basic views of this passage and every known Christian Church holds to one of them (or a mixing of them). Briefly, they are:

- *The historic pre-millennial view* – This doctrine says that after Christ returns, He will reign physically on the earth for 1000 years until God brings about the new heavens and the new earth.
- *The dispensational pre-millennial view* – This doctrine says that Christ will return to take the Church out of the world before the seven years of tribulation, and will return again with the Church after the Great Tribulation is over, resurrect martyrs who have been saved and died during the days of tribulation, bind Satan, and set up an earthly kingdom that will last 1000 years. When the 1000-year reign is over then Satan will be released to tempt mankind again, but will ultimately be defeated. Following his defeat, the Great White Throne judgment will take place.
- *The post-millennial view* – This doctrine in its essence say that as the gospel is spread throughout the world, the world will eventually become evangelized, getting better and better until it reaches an idyllic state for 1000 years, just before the return of Christ. Just after the return of Christ there will be a general resurrection.
- *The a-millennial view* – This view basically says that the millennial reign of 1000 years is not to be taken literally as a perfect utopia at the end of the age, but is in fact the whole history of the Church age—from Christ's first coming until His second coming. The *"reigning"* is done by saints in heaven with Christ. His return ushers in judgment, reward, and the creation of a new earth. It is with this view in mind that this book is written.

Having started back at the beginning of the Christian age again in 19:11, we are once again going through the story from another perspective. The account has already been given as to what lies in store for evil and what the final events of the world will bring to pass. Now we find John giving the same message from yet another view. This time he uses the idea of a 1000-year reign to drive his point home. We must remember as we look at this important section of scripture that numbers are not literal in apocalyptic writings, but are symbolic in nature. We will find that the millennium has more to offer to the open mind than what we see on the surface.

Throughout this chapter John goes on with the theme of victory that he began in 19:11 when we started this sixth vision. Here is the theme—victory for the people of God, not a perfect paradise in the world. Nowhere else in the entire Bible does the idea of an earthly millennial reign occur. Only in this chapter, verses 2-7, do we come across this controversial idea. If verses 4-6 had not been written as a part of this chapter, no one would ever have dreamed of a literal earthly 1000 years of Christ reigning on the earth. To build one's whole theology and philosophy of the end times on three highly symbolic verses seems to be a very dangerous thing to do. The most natural division of this chapter seems to be as follows:

1. Satan is bound (vv. 1-3).
2. The souls of the dead in Christ reign with Christ (vv. 4-6).
3. The final battle between good and evil (vv. 7-10).
4. The resurrection and final judgment (vv. 11-15).

King of Kings - Forever!

I saw heaven standing open and there before me was a white horse, whose rider is called Faithful and True. With justice he judges and makes war. His eyes are like blazing fire, and on his head are many crowns. He has a name written on him that no one knows but he himself. He is dressed in a robe dipped in blood, and his name is the Word of God. The armies of heaven were following him, riding on white horses and dressed in fine linen, white and clean. Out of his mouth comes a sharp sword with which to strike down the nations. "He will rule them with an iron scepter." He treads the winepress of the fury of the wrath of God Almighty. On his robe and on his thigh he has this name written: KING OF KINGS AND LORD OF LORDS. (19:11-16)

From the first chapter of this book 1:7 onward we see the story unfolding of the return of the Christ who is coming in power and glory. In these few verses the sentiment is echoed again. We see Him in chapter fourteen as the reaper of the earth and earlier in this chapter we see Him as the Bridegroom. The image that we see now however is one of Jesus as the great military leader. The opening of heaven brings the idea of a sudden appearing in glorious fashion. Pieces of pictures that we have seen in various parts of this book are used to describe our mighty Savior. He is called "Faithful and True," just as He was in the letter to Thyatira (2:18). His eyes are like fire as we saw in 1:14 and 2:18. He is said to be wearing many crowns, signifying His Lordship over all the crowned heads of the earth. His clothes are stained with the blood of His conquered enemies (as from the winepress in 14:14-20). Those following Him are dressed in pure linen and not in battle garb because the battle is the Lord's—and He is already the victor! The blood and appearance of the conquering rider is pure, signifying one who is truly King and will reign forever. We see the sharp sword coming out of His mouth again as we did in 1:16 as the reminder that He truly rules. It's a picture of now and forever.

The Horrible End

And I saw an angel standing in the sun, who cried in a loud voice to all the birds flying in midair, "Come, gather together for the great supper of God, so that you may eat the flesh of kings, generals, and mighty men, of horses and their riders, and the flesh of all people, free and slave, small and great." Then I saw the beast and the kings of the earth and their armies gathered together to make war against the rider on the horse and his army. But the beast was captured, and with him the false prophet who had performed the miraculous signs on his behalf. With these signs he had deluded those who had received the mark of the beast and worshiped his image. The two of them were thrown alive into the fiery lake of burning sulfur. The rest of them were killed with the sword that came out of the mouth of the rider on the horse, and all the birds gorged themselves on their flesh. (19:17-21)

This passage is sometimes referred to as *the feast of the birds*. This is a marked contrast to the wedding supper of the Lamb and is the result of the battle of Armageddon. Another angel is seen standing in the bright sunlight above the earth and calling to all the birds to join in the feast of the flesh of the rebellious against God. Again we see in symbolic terms the battle for men's souls reenacted and the cohorts of the devil defeated and destroyed once and for all. One thing is sure however, and that is the fact that the Lord will have the last word and His enemies will all be defeated—never to rise again—when He comes to gather His Church to be with Him. All humanity takes part in one of these two spiritual meals. We will either be present at the feast of the birds and destroyed by sin, or we will take part in the marriage supper of the Lamb.

The reality of hell is portrayed here and we must take is seriously. For just as John could not put the wonders, the beauty, and the glory of heaven into accurate words, neither can he describe the final judgment of God. Rebellion against God leads to eternal death. Fire and brimstone cannot begin to describe the horribleness of the end of those who rebel against God.

The Thousand-Year Punishment

And I saw an angel coming down out of heaven, having the key to the Abyss and holding in his hand a great chain. He seized the dragon, that ancient serpent, who is the devil, or Satan, and bound him for a thousand years. He threw him into the Abyss, and locked and sealed it over him, to keep him from deceiving the nations anymore until the thousand years were ended. After that, he must be set free for a short time. (20:1-3)

We now confront another angel. He is coming from heaven, but his destination is not the earth. He has not only a key to the Abyss, but a chain by which he binds Satan. This is not necessarily punishment, but a method of confinement to keep him from his full reign of terror. The angel is said to grab the devil, tie him up with the chain and lock him in the Abyss for 1000 years.

We must realize the symbolic implications in what is being said here. First of all, the number 1000 is simply a way of describing a large number. Numbers are used figuratively in the scriptures, such as in Psalm 50:10 where God is said to own the cattle on 1000 hills. Does anyone really think that God just owns 1000 hills worth of cattle and the rest belong to someone else? Job tells us that man is not wise enough to answer God once in 1000 times. No doubt we would find ourselves limited even more than that. Just as the Hebrew phrase of "forty days and forty nights" means a long time and is not meant to be specific, this concept of 1000 years is longer, but also an indefinite period of time. Ten is the symbolic number of completeness (ten fingers, ten toes, Ten Commandments, etc.). Ten cubed shows the completeness of time for mankind. Satan is bound for the period of the Church age.

It is foolish and unnecessary to try to make something bigger and more mysterious than it is. God wins; Satan loses. That's the story!

The Enemy is Bound

And I saw an angel coming down out of heaven, having the key to the Abyss and holding in his hand a great chain. He seized the dragon, that ancient serpent, who is the devil, or Satan, and bound him for a thousand years. He threw him into the Abyss, and locked and sealed it over him, to keep him from deceiving the nations anymore until the thousand years were ended. After that, he must be set free for a short time. (20:1-3 cont.)

We see no mention in this passage about a *rapture* of the Church preceding these events—or anywhere else in this chapter (or even in the whole Bible) for that manner. What we have here is John once more taking us behind the scenes to bring a message of hope to the Christian age.

The key to the Abyss is symbolic, as is the chain, for you cannot tie up a spirit with a chain. Though Satan is at work in the world, his activities have been limited and curtailed. He cannot destroy the Church because of the limitations God has put on him. At the end of time he will be released for an all out effort of evil, but for the present age he is bound. Jesus saw Satan "falling like lightning from heaven" (Luke 10:18). Satan is bound! He cannot stop the establishment of the Church in this world. To understand how bound Satan is, remember that he could not even hurt a hog without the permission of Jesus (Mark 5:11-13). Mark 3:27 also relates that no one can enter a strong man's house and spoil his goods unless the strong man is first bound. Satan is the bound one.

Christ is reigning with those who have already passed over from this life and He is in complete control. What a wonderful message of comfort and hope for the Church of John's day and ours as well! There is no reason for any Christian to ever fear Satan and the hold he has over this world. He may tempt us, but he cannot make us fall. Because of Jesus Christ, Satan is a defeated foe already!

Grace for the Journey

I saw thrones on which were seated those who had been given authority to judge. And I saw the souls of those who had been beheaded because of their testimony for Jesus and because of the word of God. They had not worshiped the beast or his image and had not received his mark on their foreheads or their hands. They came to life and reigned with Christ a thousand years. (The rest of the dead did not come to life until the thousand years were ended.) This is the first resurrection. Blessed and holy are those who have part in the first resurrection. The second death has no power over them, but they will be priests of God and of Christ and will reign with him for a thousand years. (20:4-6)

John makes no implication that the saints are reigning in an earthly kingdom. Those who are absent from the body are present with the Lord (II Corinthians 5:6-7). That is the message that John is trying to give. John teaches only a bodily resurrection and it comes at the time of the second coming of Christ. The Westminster Catechism states:

The souls of believers are at their death made perfect in holiness, and do immediately pass into glory; and their bodies, being still united to Christ, do yet rest in their graves till the resurrection.

Those who have already passed over—in Christ—have no fear of the second death, the lake of fire. This is the "hell" that we hear sermons about and though we do not doubt its reality, it poses no threat for the child of God. Satan is a defeated foe and we are a redeemed people. When we leave this world we are transported into a great and glorious one.

There are so many Christians who live with a fear of dying or are afraid of what they may face when they finally stand before God. There is no reason to live that way. If we have trusted Christ for our salvation and count on His grace to take us through this life then we can count on that same grace to keep us when we reach the other side.

The End of the Enemy

When the thousand years are over, Satan will be released from his prison and will go out to deceive the nations in the four corners of the earth—Gog and Magog—to gather them for battle. In number they are like the sand on the seashore. They marched across the breadth of the earth and surrounded the camp of God's people, the city he loves. But fire came down from heaven and devoured them. And the devil, who deceived them, was thrown into the lake of burning sulfur, where the beast and the false prophet had been thrown. They will be tormented day and night for ever and ever. (20:7-10)

Here is a picture of the final battle between good and evil. Gog and Magog are symbols of an empire that was taken from Ezekiel 38-39. Gog is a prince and Magog is his domain. Throughout Jewish literature these names become symbolic for the enemies of Israel and now they are revealed to us as enemies of the Church. We are often tempted to point to events around us and say that this is Satan's final blow, but we must be careful to remember that Jesus said that no one knows when His coming would be. The "When" in verse seven is the Greek word, "Hotan," which means, "Whenever." This puts the whole event of Satan's uprising in an indefinite time frame. When it does happen, it will be the same battle that was mentioned in 16:13-16.

The fire from heaven is symbolic of the second coming of Christ and that event puts an end to Satan's power once and for all. He is thrown into the lake of fire and is eternally condemned.

This is the end for the tempter of our souls. He has fallen from the heights of heaven to the earth and his end will be in the lake of fire that never burns out. Though the Bible doesn't give us a lot of details pertaining to this punishment, we can easily understand that it is a judgment that is meant to be fierce and meant to be complete. In the end, the enemy of our souls gets his just desserts.

The End of Unbelief

Then I saw a great white throne and him who was seated on it. Earth and sky fled from his presence, and there was no place for them. And I saw the dead, great and small, standing before the throne, and books were opened. Another book was opened, which is the book of life. The dead were judged according to what they had done as recorded in the books. The sea gave up the dead that were in it, and death and Hades gave up the dead that were in them, and each person was judged according to what he had done. Then death and Hades were thrown into the lake of fire. The lake of fire is the second death. If anyone's name was not found written in the book of life, he was thrown into the lake of fire. (20:11-15)

Earth and sky are destroyed at the judgment seat of God. The newly resurrected man must have a new uncorrupted world. The new earth is a greatly overlooked promise for the future of the Church. All this is in keeping with the whole tenor of scripture as found in Psalm 102:25-27; Isaiah 51:6; Mark 13:31; and II Peter 3:10. Christ said that His kingdom was spiritual and not of this world. The whole idea of a physical reign was rejected by every part of His earthly ministry.

The idea of a book of life is also found throughout scripture: Exodus 32:32; Psalm 69:28; Isaiah 4:3; Philippians 4:3; and Revelation 3:5; 13:8. When all the events of this world come down to the end, people will either enjoy eternity in the presence of the Lord, or spend a timeless end in the lake of fire.

What we know about heaven and hell is often tainted by popular culture, secular literature, or by what some preacher has proclaimed from his or her pulpit. Some images we pick up have validity and some just plainly do not. What we find in scripture must be interpreted honestly and in context if we are to begin to gain an understanding of the world to come. Here we see reward for the faithful and punishment for the unbelieving. That's all we really need to know.

The Seventh Vision: Revelation 21:1–22:5

The final vision tells of last things. The earth is transformed into the paradise that God has intended it to be from the beginning. The people of God begin their eternal abode with Christ and there is an end to all suffering, pain, and sorrow. The bride (the Church) and the groom (Christ) are finally joined and enter into a marriage of joy forever.

The images of the city are representative description of the people of God in this union. Built upon the foundation of the apostles and surrounded by the example of the Old Testament people of God, they have a beauty that John describes at great length.

Everything is made new as it was in the Garden of Eden. Nothing impure is there, but the righteous will abide with God in harmony forever.

Peace at Last

Then I saw a new heaven and a new earth, for the first heaven and the first earth had passed away, and there was no longer any sea. (21:1)

John witnesses the appearance of a new heaven and a new earth, but he is not seeing the end of this present world and universe. What he is referring to is the fact that since sin and all of its adherents are now out of the picture, the earth will be regaining Paradise, for the old order of things has now passed away. The redeemed of God will now live forever in their transformed home with Christ. This brings to fulfillment the prophecy of Isaiah 65:17, where he records the Lord saying, "Behold, I will create new heavens and a new earth. The former things will not be remembered, nor will they come to mind." Isaiah 66:22 also speaks of "…the new heavens and the new earth…" that will endure before the Lord. It is a time of forgetting sorrow, saying goodbye to sin, and the beginning of an eternity of walking in the light of God. II Peter 3:13 also makes reference to this, "But in keeping with his promise we are looking forward to a new heaven and a new earth, the home of righteousness."

The phrase concerning the seas is one of symbolism. Since the earth is mostly covered with water, it is hard to imagine what it would be like without the seas. It wouldn't seem much like a place of joy to those who had sailed the seas their whole natural life, only to find that eternity would make them a "landlubber." The sea, as we have seen earlier, was always a threat to the Jewish mind. It was the abiding place of one of this book's terrible beasts. What John means is that all is now peace and joy. All the frightening things that the sea stood for are no longer present. God's people will be at peace throughout all eternity.

Home at Last

I saw the Holy City, the new Jerusalem, coming down out of heaven from God, prepared as a bride beautifully dressed for her husband. And I heard a loud voice from the throne saying, "Now the dwelling of God is with men, and he will live with them. They will be his people, and God himself will be with them and be their God. He will wipe every tear from their eyes. There will be no more death or mourning or crying or pain, for the old order of things has passed away." He who was seated on the throne said, "I am making everything new!" Then he said, "Write this down, for these words are trustworthy and true." (21:2-5)

John also sees a city, but this is not a material city made by man. It is a city of people; it is the host of the redeemed. It is the bride of Christ and it is coming, not down to the earth, but to where Christ is. No longer will the bride and Bridegroom be kept separate, but now they will forever be truly one. We have already seen this in 14:3-4.

A voice from the throne declares the words every Christian longs to hear. We will live in the presence of God. We will eternally belong to Him and He will provide for us. No longer will we have to endure tears, sorrow, pain, or death. A new order of things will have come to pass and replaced all that we had to withstand as the result of the effect of sin. Certainly, in this world we will have to face suffering, disappointment, and even possible persecution and death. But in the world to come there will be a wedding and after this wedding there will truly be a happy-ever-after ending.

Again a message comes from the throne. This time it is clearly from God Himself and He declares that the new order, the new creation, and the new age have begun. John is instructed to record what he hears so that others may benefit from this message. It is true and it will not change. The Word of God is the one thing that will endure forever.

The Second Death

He said to me: "It is done. I am the Alpha and the Omega, the Beginning and the End. To him who is thirsty I will give to drink without cost from the spring of the water of life. He who overcomes will inherit all this, and I will be his God and he will be my son. But the cowardly, the unbelieving, the vile, the murderers, the sexually immoral, those who practice magic arts, the idolaters and all liars–their place will be in the fiery lake of burning sulfur. This is the second death." (21:6-8)

The message from God continues. No doubt this message is intended for the Church. God declares that He is the beginning and the end of all things. "Alpha" is the first letter in the Greek alphabet and "Omega" is the last. This is a way of saying that none came before God and there will be no one or nothing after Him. We can receive everlasting life—that is, it will start at one point and go on forever, but God is not everlasting; He is eternal. Not only is there no end to Him, but also there is no starting point either. He has always been and always will be and He promises everlasting life for all who overcome the hardships and sin of this present age. Such a person will belong solely to God and receive all the privileges of being His child.

A warning is given however, that it is only the pure who receive such a reward. Sinners—and the list is clear, "the cowardly, the unbelievers, the vile, murderers, the sexually immoral, magicians, idolaters, and liars," will spend their everlasting life in the lake of fire. This second death must be avoided at all costs. Everything is at stake. The word to the Church is that they must endure to the end.

This is the message of Jesus throughout this entire book. In its essence we find that the Church will experience trials in this age, but if it perseveres and overcomes it will be rewarded. It doesn't get much clearer than that.

Here Comes the Bride

One of the seven angels who had the seven bowls full of the seven last plagues came and said to me, "Come, I will show you the bride, the wife of the Lamb." And he carried me away in the Spirit to a mountain great and high, and showed me the Holy City, Jerusalem, coming down out of heaven from God. It shone with the glory of God, and its brilliance was like that of a very precious jewel, like a jasper, clear as crystal. It had a great, high wall with twelve gates, and with twelve angels at the gates. On the gates were written the names of the twelve tribes of Israel. There were three gates on the east, three on the north, three on the south and three on the west. The wall of the city had twelve foundations, and on them were the names of the twelve apostles of the Lamb. (21:9-14)

As we meet an angel whom we had met earlier, John is taken on a tour. We must remember however, that what John sees is not a physical city. This city is the people, just as the Church is not a building, but a people. The host of the redeemed is the wife of Christ. We will one day be united with Him as a bride to her groom. It may be a hard concept to grasp, but it need not be. John is describing the redeemed of the ages, not a physical city, who is one with God because they have shared in the life of Christ. The city is the host of the redeemed of all history, not just at the end of the age.

John gives a great description of the city, but we must look at this city with spiritual eyes, not physical. Each part of the description has a meaning. God is the light of this body of believers and John is dazzled by His glory. The Lord's bride is as beautiful as jewels and more precious in value. The walls represent the security of God's people in His presence. Within the walls are twelve gates, which represent the way of salvation. In John's mind, the Old and New Testaments represent the people of God. Here we see the twelve apostles, built upon the foundation of the twelve tribes as the way into the city. Angels are not to bar the way to Paradise, but to usher in all who will come.

The Measurement of Holiness

The angel who talked with me had a measuring rod of gold to measure the city, its gates and its walls. The city was laid out like a square, as long as it was wide. He measured the city with the rod and found it to be 12,000 stadia in length, and as wide and high as it is long. He measured its wall and it was 144 cubits thick, by man's measurement, which the angel was using. The wall was made of jasper, and the city of pure gold, as pure as glass. The foundations of the city walls were decorated with every kind of precious stone. The first foundation was jasper, the second sapphire, the third chalcedony, the fourth emerald, the fifth sardonyx, the sixth carnelian, the seventh chrysolite, the eighth beryl, the ninth topaz, the tenth chrysoprase, the eleventh jacinth, and the twelfth amethyst. The twelve gates were twelve pearls, each gate made of a single pearl. The great street of the city was of pure gold, like transparent glass. I did not see a temple in the city, because the Lord God Almighty and the Lamb are its temple. The city does not need the sun or the moon to shine on it, for the glory of God gives it light, and the Lamb is its lamp. (21:15-23)

Now we see John talking with an angel who is about to do some measuring. The idea comes from Ezekiel 40:3ff and 42:15-20. The idea of both Ezekiel and John is to show a difference between what is holy and what is common. To the ancient mind, the cube was the symbol of perfection. There is no significance in the literal numbers given here. It is simply perfect. The people of God have come through great tribulation and have been purified by the blood of the Lamb. The stones and gold of verses eighteen through twenty-one give the picture of beauty, richness, and splendor. They are spiritual qualities and realities. Holiness is not only of great value; it is also expensive.

John didn't see a temple because God and the Lamb are there. The whole place in the presence of the Almighty is a holy of holies. There is no need for the sun because the Light of the World is there.

That's a lesson we can take to the bank. If we have the Lord we don't need anything else. He is not called the "Alpha" and "Omega" for nothing.

The Most Important Book of All

The nations will walk by its light, and the kings of the earth will bring their splendor into it. On no day will its gates ever be shut, for there will be no night there. The glory and honor of the nations will be brought into it. Nothing impure will ever enter it, nor will anyone who does what is shameful or deceitful, but only those whose names are written in the Lamb's book of life. (21:24-27)

It is said "…nations will walk by its light and the kings of the earth will bring their splendor into it." This is another way of saying that the call of the gospel is universal. The gates into the family of God (the New Jerusalem) are never closed. This is also more proof that John is not recording this book in chronological order because even though the final judgment has taken place, the nations are still present. It also shows us that the New Jerusalem is not the final resting place of the saints as it is popularly, but unscripturally thought. This is a city of people—the people of God—just as the Church is not a building, but the people of God. The righteous will make up that city and anyone who is not made righteous will not be a part of it. The unclean will not walk the highway of holiness (Isaiah 35:8-10), but only those who have been recorded in the Lamb's book of Life.

What this means is that it truly does make a difference as to how we live in this world. In fact, according to what we read here, this world is simply a preparation room for the next world. We will receive for eternity what we have earned here in mortality. That's why we should make sure that nothing comes between our Lord and us. Nothing should abate our devotion; nothing can be allowed to interfere with our relationship with the Divine. There is no prize higher than being recorded in the Master's book of life.

The Light of the World

Then the angel showed me the river of the water of life, as clear as crystal, flowing from the throne of God and of the Lamb down the middle of the great street of the city. On each side of the river stood the tree of life, bearing twelve crops of fruit, yielding its fruit every month. And the leaves of the tree are for the healing of the nations. No longer will there be any curse. The throne of God and of the Lamb will be in the city, and his servants will serve him. They will see his face, and his name will be on their foreheads. There will be no more night. They will not need the light of a lamp or the light of the sun, for the Lord God will give them light. And they will reign for ever and ever. (22:1-5)

For the last part of the vision, we find John leading us from the idea of the make-up of this city to the blessings of being a part of it. The Bible opens in the book of *Genesis* with man losing Paradise. Revelation closes its final vision with man regaining it. Everything that was once lost—and even more—will be restored as man is perfectly restored with God. The new world with Christ is a world of abundant life. It is symbolized through phrases like "water of life" and a "tree of life"—which is constantly bearing fruit. The nations are healed, there is no more sickness, and the curse that fell on the earth as a result of Adam's fall has been revoked.

Most importantly, God is there and we will serve Him. We will see Him face to face and His seal will be upon us. To be in the presence of the Lord is not to be in a state of idleness. We may not be sure of many things concerning the next life, but the Bible is clear that it is a place of song and joyful service to the Lord. The Light of the World will shine forever and the saints of God will reign with Him forever.

This is the end of the final vision that John receives. It ends on a high note. He has told the story seven times and God always wins—and He always will!

Epilogue - Revelation 22:6-11

We have come to the end of the seven visions and now John caps his writing with the promise that all he has said is true and that Jesus is truly coming to make it all come to pass. He is told to publish these tidings and warn people that the time to prepare for Christ's return is now. The First and the Last has spoken and there can be no change in the plan. All who are righteous will reign with Christ forever and those who are not will be left outside the eternal kingdom of God in a place of horrific punishment.

John closes with the invitation for Christ to come back. He is ready to see His Master and the promise is given again that He is coming soon.

The message of the book of *Revelation* is best understood as follows: In this world the Church will have trouble and sorrow as they work to fulfill the Great Commission. However, the believers should stand firm, for the King of the Church has not forgotten her. We are to hold fast to Christ and His teachings – for in the end, we win! The glories that await the faithful in the presence of God will make our brief time of suffering here worth it all.

Worship the Lord Alone

The angel said to me, "These words are trustworthy and true. The Lord, the God of the spirits of the prophets, sent his angel to show his servants the things that must soon take place." "Behold, I am coming soon! Blessed is he who keeps the words of the prophecy in this book." I, John, am the one who heard and saw these things. And when I had heard and seen them, I fell down to worship at the feet of the angel who had been showing them to me. But he said to me, "Do not do it! I am a fellow servant with you and with your brothers the prophets and of all who keep the words of this book. Worship God!" (22:6-9)

We have come to the end of the seven visions of this book. John now closes his writings with a promise of the coming of Jesus. That fact is the most important theme in this whole book. Jesus is portrayed as glorified in the first chapter, He is the figure the book revolves around, and He is the soon coming King! Of this we are sure and all else is commentary and will be worked out in His own way and on His own time schedule. We see Jesus from cover to cover in the midst of the Church and in the place of the victor. Our hope is in Him. Nothing else matters.

The words given are much like what we see in the prologue. The angel verifies that all that has been given is true and can be relied upon. The same God that inspired the prophets of old has now used His angel to inspire the events at hand.

The words of Jesus never cease to thrill us. He is coming again and the time will be soon. The sixth beatitude of this book is a blessing pronounced upon those who will pay attention to these words. John then puts his own personal stamp on this writing and once again we see him instructed not to worship what was created—no matter how dazzling—but the Creator only. This is not bad advice in our day of materialism.

The Focus of the Book

Then he told me, "Do not seal up the words of the prophecy of this book, because the time is near. Let him who does wrong continue to do wrong; let him who is vile continue to be vile; let him who does right continue to do right; and let him who is holy continue to be holy." "Behold, I am coming soon! My reward is with me, and I will give to everyone according to what he has done. I am the Alpha and the Omega, the First and the Last, the Beginning and the End. "Blessed are those who wash their robes, that they may have the right to the tree of life and may go through the gates into the city. Outside are the dogs, those who practice magic arts, the sexually immoral, the murderers, the idolaters and everyone who loves and practices falsehood. "I, Jesus, have sent my angel to give you this testimony for the churches. I am the Root and the Offspring of David, and the bright Morning Star." (22:10-16)

The words of this prophecy are to be published. This is just the opposite of what Daniel was told (Daniel 8:26; 12:4, 9). What John saw is not for the future, but is right at hand. The time of the opening of the sealed book is already upon us. We are experiencing it now.

Verse eleven gives us a summary of all that is contained in the message of this book. The wicked will be wicked and the righteous will be righteous, but each will receive what he has earned at the coming of the Lord. His coming will not be long. Jesus refers to Himself in the same terms that we use to describe the eternal God on the throne (20:11; 21:6). They are one and the same.

Another blessing is given for those who endure and overcome so that they can make up the city of God. Those who are a part of the city are holy, but those who are not are the enemies of God.

It was Jesus who began the book and now closes the book and we need to make no mistake about His identity. He is the Leader of the Church, the Messiah of Israel, and the Sunrise of the Day of the Lord. He is our soon coming King and worthy forever to be praised.

Come!

The Spirit and the bride say, "Come!" And let him who hears say, "Come!" Whoever is thirsty, let him come; and whoever wishes, let him take the free gift of the water of life. I warn everyone who hears the words of the prophecy of this book: If anyone adds anything to them, God will add to him the plagues described in this book. And if anyone takes words away from this book of prophecy, God will take away from him his share in the tree of life and in the holy city, which are described in this book. He who testifies to these things says, "Yes, I am coming soon." Amen. Come, Lord Jesus. The grace of the Lord Jesus be with God's people. Amen. (22:17-21)

A series of invitations are given to those who would read this book. There is still time to get right with God and John the revelator becomes John the evangelist for one last appeal. He also warns one more time of the seriousness of this decision. Life everlasting is at stake. Heaven or hell is still the only eternal options for mankind.

The readers are warned not to mess with what is written here. Naturally, what John is referring to is this book in particular and not the whole of scripture, although his warning is good advice for the Bible in general. God's Word is holy and should be honored as the ultimate truth.

The last words of Jesus give us a sure promise of His return. John, as all Christians should, looks forward to that day. It may seem that the coming of the Lord is just a story because of the length of time from John's words to the present. However, we are still required as Christians to walk and live by faith and not by sight. Jesus will not desert us. He will not go back on His word. There will be a wedding of the Divine Groom and His earthly bride. We will be joined with Him forever and we will be forever in praise to Him. John was grateful. May we experience the grace of God to have the same attitude!

Parting Thoughts

We have come to the end of the Book of Revelation itself and no doubt there have been some thoughts with which you have disagreed, some that have confirmed your faith, and some that made you reexamine long-held beliefs. Obviously because of the brevity of this book and because of its devotional content, it is far from exhaustive. The book is a book of hope, however, for the people of God of all time. John's visions in this book all point to the Christ, Jesus the Lamb of God, who takes away the sins of the world. That is what I have attempted to do as well.

No doubt this a-millennial approach will produce a reaction from those who have been raised and trained to believe in a more chronological and sensational method of interpretation to this literature. Still, where we may disagree in places I hope we can agree on the following five things:

1. Jesus is coming again. No man knows the day or the hour, but as sure as the Bible is true, He is coming back for His own.
2. When He comes He will balance the scales of injustice.
3. At His coming every knee will bow before Him and proclaim Him as Lord.
4. Those who have chosen to reject Him in this life will be rejected by Him in the life to come.
5. Those who have dedicated themselves to Him in this life will enter eternally into the joys of their Lord.

I hope to meet you at that great praise party and we can discuss this more fully. Be blessed and be a blessing until that day!

LaVergne, TN USA
04 June 2010
184977LV00002B/3/P